The Fourth Child
Glimpses of Twentieth Century Bengali Poetry

Prabir Das

Jointly Published By

8 Sages Entertainment
St. Louis, Missouri, USA

Society for Healing Arts & Diversity Enrichment
Houston, Texas, USA

Distributed by

প্রতিভাষ PRATIVASH

18/A Gobinda Mondal Road, Kolkata 700 002, West Bengal, India.

The Fourth Child
Glimpses of Twentieth Century Bengali Poetry

The Fourth Child
A collection of transcreated twentieth century Bengali poetry

Transcreation, Photography and Cover Design
Prabir Das
Photographs of the poets are collected from resources available freely on the internet

Illustration and Design
Debasish Bardhan

Production Control
Subrata Basu

Page Setting
Samir Kumar Dey

First Published On
April 25, 2018

Printing and Binding by
Anderson Printing House Pvt. Ltd. Kolkata, India

Jointly Published by
Society for Healing Arts and Diversity Enrichment, Houston, Texas, USA
8 Sages Entertainment, St. Louis, Missouri, USA

Distributed by
Prativash, 18/A, Gobinda Mondal Road, Kolkata - 700 002, West Bengal, India, P: 33 2557 8659

Copyright © 2018, Prabir Das. All rights reserved.
All rights reserved. No part of this publication may be reproduced, distributed, or transmitted in any form or by any means, including photocopying, recording, or other electronic or mechanical methods, without the prior written permission of the author/translator.

ISBN 978-0-692-08499-1
Library of Congress Control Number: 2018903315

Acknowledgment

Arundhati Subramaniam	Mihir Chakrabarty
Ayananshu Banerjee	Nirendranath Chakraborty
Bharabi Das	Prasanta K Saha (PK Saha)
Buddhadeb Chattopadhyay	Ranadhir Mitra
Jishnu Dey	Sampurna Chattarji
Joy Goswami	Shankha Ghosh
Kaberi Dutta	Suvo Das Gupta
Krishnakali Roy	Swati Gangopadhyay
Meenakshi Chattopadhyay	Tridib Chattopadhyay

Other Works by Prabir Das

Aasoley Eti Ekti Bijnapan
(*This is Actually a Propaganda*)
A collection of short stories in Bengali

Keyartekarer Preyasi
(*Caretaker's Beloved*)
A collection of plays in Bengali

Pellucid Proem
A Candid Exposure of Polychromatic Feelings
(A book of photography and narration)

Prattuttarey Aatmohatya O Aatmohatyaar Prattuttarey
(*Retorted through Self-Slaughter and in Retort of the Self-Slaughtered*)
A short experimental film

Authored Plays

Bengali
Anatikrom (*Unsurpassable*)
Living Room
Naatokey Naatok (*Theatre of Theatre*)
Keyartekarer Preyasi (*Caretaker's Beloved*)
Ananda Sen (*Ananda Sen is a Bengali name*)
Chalabat Jaromaan (*Kinetic Inertia*)
Aphrodite O Tantalus (*Aphrodite and Tantalus*)
Shikhandee (*Shikhandee is a character from the epic of Mahabharta*)
Sanket (*The Signal*)
Poter Bibi (*Painter's Woman*)

English
Celebrated Silence: Authored jointly with Dr. Anisha Singh
Duryodhana - The Unconquerable

To

Goirick Angon Das

You motivated me to initiate this book. Your quest in your root as well as in its heritage inspired me to dare. I thought I was unworthy of challenging myself to savor the intricacy of modern Bengali poetry in English. Your passionate thirst to embrace your origin humbled me. Hence...

In this twenty-first century twenty-one selected Bengali poetries on your twenty-first birthday.

I am thankful, my son.

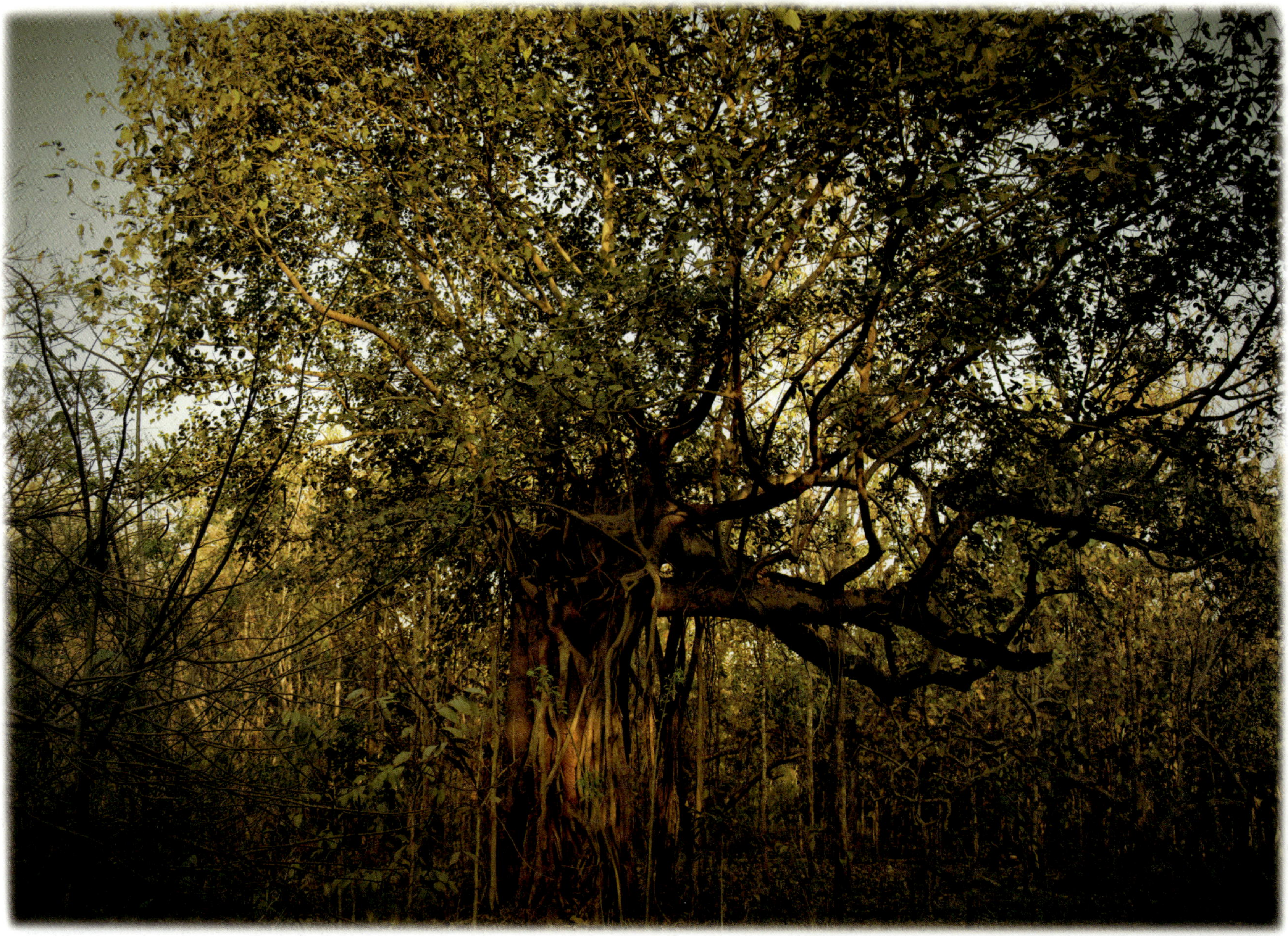

PRELUDE

Love towards poetry is polarized. Either one loves it deeply or remains detached. In between exists a bridge that is seldom crossed. I did cross this bridge nearly four decades ago in my teens, never to return to the other side again. Poetry flows freely underneath this bridge, inviting all to take a dip in it. I invite you to this stream.

For many moons I didn't swim. I only remained on the banks sunbathing. I turned into a lotus eater, a lotophagi. A few months ago, my soon to be twenty-one year old son, Goirick, out of the blue, engaged me in a conversation. He uttered names of Bengali stalwarts like Upendrakishore Ray Chowdhury and Sukumar Ray. I am an expatriated Bengali domiciled in the United States of America for nearly three decades. Hence, Goirick was born in this country. I failed to nourish him with Bengali literature, our root.

Though fluent in speaking, due to my negligence, Goirick was never privileged to read or write in Bengali. This pleasant shock of discussion soon felt like a heavenly pinch once he advanced the conversation referencing Buddhadeb Bosu, another lusty jewel of Bengali poetry and literature. How could he know these names? I couldn't help but appreciate Goirick's insuppressible zeal towards digging into his root.

Through this emotionally surreal conversation, the thought of translation popped up in my head. I felt, there must be many more children just like Goirick, who crave to touch the essence of Bengal, especially through its literature. Many non-Bengali Indians and non-Indians perhaps wish to be included as well. I began the self-assumed daunting task without ever promising myself or anyone towards its possible culmination. Months later, unlike many of my unfinished works, I am pleased to extend this collection, glimpsing Bengali poetry of the 20th century, to all who wish to swim in the estuary. My humble effort in this book awaits to quench their thirst, though may be just by a tiny sip.

I don't claim to be a poet, nor am I an audacious translator. Connoisseurs of poetry, through their ability to create, become omnipotent like a god in poetics. However, often they are erratically egoist. I fear their possible fingering towards flaws in my translation, but I find them not intolerable. Poets are often children and their tantrum naked. Similarly, in their poetry, they attempt to squeeze out the oozing truth of emotion until its last drop.

It wasn't easy to select the poetries for translation. It was a difficult process for various reasons. I have been away from the mainland of Bengal for very long and do not have access to all the Bengali poetries. Internet, in this case, turned out to be a worthless resource. Libraries in the United States do not stock Bengali poetry books. And no bookseller can survive selling just Bengali poetry books in a foreign land. A very small fragment of expatriated Bengali population read Bengali literature. Though I have a considerable volume of Bengali poetry in my possession, however, collectively it is less than a drop in the ocean of Bengali poetry. Besides, Bengali poetry is ever evolving and creating a different identity ceaselessly. Moreover, despite being a student of English literature and language, I think in Bengali as well as dream in Bengali. It is quite evident in this collection. Throughout my career as a freelance journalist (in the 1980s while I was still in Kolkata, West Bengal), I wrote only in Bengali. Subsequently I penned all my plays and other literary works only in Bengali. It was only in 2014, for the first time I began to write in English and have continued ever since.

I wished to bring forth the distinct evolution of Bengali poetry through this collection. In my selection I followed a structured madness. According to the history of Bengali language, Bengali itself was never a primary or original language. It was a dialect. In his book on history of Bengali literature, Dr. Sukumar Sen (one of the most trusted or regarded Bengali linguists) wrote, 'prior to the 18th century, Bengali language didn't have any specific name or title.' It used to be identified as "Deshi" (indigenous), "Loukik" (customary), or "Praakrito" (pertaining to the populace). Even during the first half of the 19th century, Bengali language was known as "Gouriyo" or "GauDiya" (D here pronounced as deep R) bhaasaa or language of GauD (GouR). Bengal used to be known as GauD. First documentation of Bengali as a language can be traced back to as recent as 1842. Since then, the language has gone through enormous transformation. During the British era in India, Bengali language went through significant evolution. It is comparable to the European renaissance of the 16th century, though the renaissance in Bengal went through tougher challenges due to its colonization at the time. Bengal renaissance perhaps began with Ram Mohan Roy (1772 – 1833) and ended with Rabindranath Tagore (1861 – 1941). During this period, besides language, Bengal's culture, societal outlook, rituals, beliefs and many other areas metamorphosed. Bengali language prior to Tagore appears to be somewhat of a riddle even for contemporary Bengalis. The feudalism of elites contributed towards enhancement of the language but kept it away from the masses. Therefore, the common people, on daily basis communicated in one language and the elite authors wrote in heavier words and sentences that remained incomprehensible by the majority. I omitted poetries from that era.

Rabindranath Tagore, himself was an institution. He still dominates Bengali literature. Tagore and his creations were kept hostage by Visva Bharati (or Biswa-Bharati) and its staunch affiliates until copyright expired in 2001. Once it freed itself from the cages of the puritans, it began to become universal. Tagore himself translated a vast portion of his literary creation. Later, others have taken successful initiatives as well. The contemporaries of Tagore, such as Ishwar Chandra Gupta (1812 – 1859), Madhusudan Dutta (1824 – 1873), Nabinchandra Sen (1847 – 1909), Jatindramohan Bagchi (1878 – 1948), Dwijendralal Roy (1863 – 1913), Satyendranath Dutta (1882 – 1922), Mohitlal Majumdar (1888 – 1952) immensely contributed to Bengali literature. Each of them had a distinct style as well as preference of content in their poetry. I kept their creation aside for another edition, if ever.

My primary focus went onto the poets of post-Tagore era. Due to the Bengal renaissance, it was obvious to find a large number of poets who aspired successfully during the 20th century. I decided to begin with Kazi Nazrul Islam and Jibananda Dash. Both were born in 1899, yet reflected two distinct different ideologies and styles through their poetries. Kazi Nazrul Islam's Bengali was ornamentally ancient comparing to the modern approach of Jibanananda Dash. Jibanananda Dash portrayed tremendously complex imageries and his choice of Bengali words was much refined. Subsequently, I picked nineteen other poets from the 20th century who were prominent. I have attempted to highlight an array of chronological transformation; Bengali poetry went through during the 20th century. The explored paths of the poets are distinctly identifiable in this collection, I believe. Nonetheless, I have kept aside many others for future, who were no less. This collection is by no means a documentation of history, geography or science of poetry. This is a simple glimpse into the Bengali poetry from the 20th century.

It is imperative to obtain knowledge of Bengal and Bengali culture, traditions and beliefs in order to relate to the content of the poetries. Whereas, Internet can be a useful resource, however, may not be complete. There is no substitute to authentic books. Knowledge knows no short cut. In any case, a profound segment of Bengal's history is often overlooked as it has somehow been degenerated. I am referring to the emotional attachment towards leftist doctrine shared by the lion share of cultural practitioners of West Bengal in the second half of the 20th century. Poets too, developed this humanitarian outlook and it is sharply reflected in their critical works. During the late sixties and early seventies, West Bengal went through a communist movement known as Naxal movement. The government at the time implemented atrocious measures that would forever remain as a disrepute imprint of ruling machinery. Political activists like Poet Saroj Dutta, whose poetry – 'Fancied Revolution of Middle-Class' is part of this collection, were connivingly murdered by the government machineries only to suppress this mass upsurge. Poets, like affiliates of any other cultural practice, reflected this sentiment in their work. Nonetheless, apart from a handful of poets, most brought forward issues of social injustice, cultural stigma, religious malpractice, psychological struggle, existential paradigm and such, including one of the most romanticized affairs of theirs, death. All of these are clearly evident in this collection.

A poet may or may not be a scholar. But his poetry must become a subject for the masses. We often assume in vain, poetry is some sort of critical work that ought to remain a subject of the so-called elites. If I am against class system, if I am against race system, I am also against acknowledging implied differences between elites and non-elites. It is a far greater obscenity than pornography for the top 1% of the population to hold onto over 80% of the wealth. It is equally obscene for a section of population to hold onto the perceived narcissism of elite supremacy. Poetry ought to be relatable to the masses, even if they are uneducated. Poetry is only as good as its reader. Like anything else in this world, poetry finds its recognition only through its readership. Otherwise, poetry has very little implication over human life. A genuine immersion in poetry can benefit societies all over. Poetry is probably the most innocent act of an adult. Poetry is non-violent. Poetry is utter truth. Poetry is adoration of philosophy. Poetry is complex but seldom complicated.

If, poetry must be a matter of the masses, then, it must discard its puritanism. Majority of the world population still suffers from poverty, scarcity of food, clothing and shelter. Education is unreachable, often a luxury for them. Poetry needs to reach them. Poetry also needs to find its way into the heart of a serial killer, a mass shooter at a school, a rapist, a groper, a thief, a liar and all other crooks of the world. Poetry could be the next best thing to therapy towards a healed, equaled and constructive universe of mankind. Forget about the meters and prosodies. Forget about the grammars, idioms and syntaxes. Just write. Just read. Just feel. And heal. Poetry is a better addiction than drug or other vices.

Bengal is known as the land of intellectuals. Though I hold serious reservation against the word 'intellectual', nonetheless, the tradition continues. Bengali language is considered to be the seventh most used language in the world. Yet its regionalism has kept it confined. I wish to break this self-imposed seclusion. Daring the possibilities of flaws, impossibilities of translating indigenous Bengali words, and my own inhibition, I have selectively opted to serve twenty-one delectable poetries of Bengal towards the readers like my son. If accepted, I will venture to dish out more, in the future.

On the path to connection between any two souls who wish to feel, stands the obnoxious barrier of words. Its severity increases by umpteen times when language itself becomes the barrier. Nonetheless, it cannot become a barricade between the Bengali poetry and the non-Bengali readers. Communication is the only desired outcome through any conversation, including poetry. Objective of this book is no different. If a Bengali as well as a non-Bengali reader can connect through the poetry in these pages, I would know, the purpose has been served.

I purposely refrained from translating the most popular poetry of any poet (except of poet Dinesh Das). Many have already translated those poetries. I salute them for their effort and creativity. I find their translation worthy. Readers of this book, I hope, would also take interest in reading those translations.

Perception is the most critical issue in any poetry. There, a moon can become a priceless pearl, a sickle or a burnt hand-rolled bread. If one doesn't have the concept of hand-rolled bread, it would be impossible to comprehend the portrayal of a hand-rolled bread through the allegory of moon. Poets can see things differently. Poets are able to aviate or dive down to the bottom of an ocean, proficient in creating a verse while sitting within a burning fire. Poets are chameleons in its supreme positive intonation. Poets are magicians. Poets are saints.

Imperatively, I stayed attuned to my inner senses as I translated Bengali poetries into English. I attempted to invoke the poet's persona in my sphere as I translated the poetry. I attempted to visualize. Words first appear as a visual to me, then hits me with its sound. I read these poetries for days before translating them. I wanted to see what the poet saw. I wanted to feel what the poet felt. As I translated, I attempted to keep the original rhythm of the poetry and each line intact. Rhythm is neither rhyme, nor the poetical prosody. Rhythm is just simply rhythm. For that, I took liberty and implanted English words that may not be the exact simple translation of the Bengali word. I rather intended to incorporate the visual, I saw. Thus, I gratefully adopted the word 'transcreation' coined by Dr. Prasanta K Saha (also known as PK Saha), a distinguished linguist in English language and literature.

It is impossible, otherwise, to translate any poetry from its original language to another. Up until poet Buddhadeb Bosu, the formation of poetries appear to be highly complex in thoughts as well as in word selections. In his poetry 'Transformation' poet Buddhadeb Bosu wrote; "Chirantaney mukti daao khanikaar amlaan khamaay," I converted it to; "Absolve eon through ungloomy condoning moment." One can argue with my choice of English words as well as their chronological placement. I confess, in that moment of translation, I transcreated exactly how I visualized the imagery. Nevertheless, I continued to replace words almost on a weekly basis, until the entire poetry appeared to be satisfactory to me. I solicited advice, guidance and support from other translators. I am thankful to them for their input and encouragement. Tomorrow or ten years down the road, these imageries may change as I evolve into a different human being. Every morning I get a new life. Every morning I become a different person. I am not static. Nor are my transcreations.

Another example I draw from poet Nirendranath Chakraborty's "Fourth Child" poetry. He wrote: "Tumio akleshey taakey ghaarey dhorey jaahaannaamey thheley ditey paaro." The imagery is complex here and the sentence construction is compound as well. Simple English translation of this line may appear something like this: You too can easily grab it by the neck/shoulder and shove it into the hell. If I write the sentence as such, it will have no poetic elegance. Therefore, I wrote; Adept you are, you can disown it easily as well.

I ask for forgiveness from all the poets, if I have applied too much of liberty.

Complexity of poetics is evident in most of the poetries I have selected for this collection. It was a challenge I tossed at myself. Not all Bengali poetries can be translated. Whereas, I would never attempt to translate a Bengali sentence like, "Tarun briddher mukh raatrey uthhey mone elo shyam shmashrumoy" (by poet Joy Goswami) (futile attempt at it would be: My mind, in the middle of the night awakened from sleep, visualizing, dark black bearded face of a man who was actually a young old…), nonetheless, poet Jibanananda Dash's "Mrittikar moto tumi aaj", I took a shot at. Mrittika is maati (deep T) or soil. Moto means alike. Tumi means you. Aaj means today. How can a human being be like soil? What did the poet intend to express through these selectively chosen words? I don't believe anyone but the poet himself, could ever express the same feeling or meaning. And when it is translated into another language, unless the relationship between the poet and the said 'soil' is comprehended, it is impossible to carry over the exact emotion. No pundit can explain the exact intention. However, many can share their individual reflection based on their own perception, none of which will ever match.

Before I ventured into this project, as an experiment, I requested four knowledgeable translators to translate one sentence from a Tagore poetry. Soon, I received four different versions. None of them were wrong, I found. They were just different. I realize, translations can never be the exact same, since, as humans, we visualize differently.

Beholden, I extend my sincerest reverence to all the poets for their benevolent attributes, enriching Bengali literature and life in general. I feel fortunate to be able to serve the poetry-loving population of the world through the glimpses of Bengali poetry. Bengali is one of the sweetest languages. Profound, prolific and proffering. Bengal (Bangladesh as well as West Bengal) is a picturesque land. Take this journey along with me. For that matter, I have included each poetry in its original form in English alphabet. The spelling of Bengali words in English alphabet doesn't adhere to any set rules and is only a casual phonetic attempt. The accompanying photographs are incorporation of my candid visuals. They are not manipulated. They are meant to be a prose and only a suggestive backdrop for the verse.

It has been my good fortune to get to know Dr. Ranadhir Mitra, son of poet Arun Mitra, who is a poet of distinction in his own right and translated many Bengali poetries in English. I am thankful and indebted to Dr. Ranadhir Mitra for his guidance and support towards this collection.

Words cannot express the gratitude I feel for my friends Debasish Bardhan and Subrata Basu for their selfless contribution and support towards publishing this collection. Back in the eighties, three of us were actively involved in all my creative endeavors including launching a little-magazine publication, publishing my first collection of short stories as well as producing my first short film. It is not just a rendezvous, decades later. It is not a mere recreation of life from our twenties. It is much more, emotions of which can never be expressed adequately in words.

Debasish Bardhan, an artist in his own right, has ably enhanced this presentation with his illustrations and design. No one could have done it better. Also, my sincere thanks and gratitude to those who have constructively and tirelessly helped to make this project a reality. They are too many to name. Their kindness towards me is inexpressible. It can only be felt. I feel. I treasure. I remain indebted.

On behalf of Society for Healing Arts and Diversity Enrichment (SHADE) and 8 Sages Entertainment, I submit this glimpses of Bengali poetry to you. My heartfelt thanks to you for your interest in Bengali poetry as well as poetry in general.

Prabir Das

February 15, 2018

Houston, Texas

A FEW WORDS ABOUT BENGAL AND BENGALI

Situated by the Bay of Bengal (Ocean), Bengal has always been a lucrative target for the opportunist rulers. Moreover, since the ancient time Bengal played a prominent role in the historic Silk Route. The Silk Route was a network of trade routes for centuries connecting the regions of Eurasia, the East and West. It stretched through the Korean peninsula and Japan to the Mediterranean Sea. The Silk Route refers to both the terrestrial and the maritime routes connecting Asia with Africa, the Middle East and southern Europe.

Existence of Bengal can be evidenced back four millennia. Ruled by dynasty after dynasty, Bengal continued to enhance its fertile glory and gained prominence through the governance of the Buddhist Pal dynasty (8th – 11th century) and Hindu Sen dynasty (11th – 12th century). Following Muslim invasions in 13th century, Bengal came under the control of Muslim Sultanates, though remained prosperous. These settling communities of traders and rulers from various parts of the world led Bengal to assimilate people of various origins and beliefs.

In the late 18th century, British entered Bengal in the guise of traders and took control of the region, eventually ruling the entire India. The readily available port of Bengal, eased their business as well as ruling. British took control of the land after winning two decisive wars - Battle of Palaasi (1757) and Battle of Buxar (1764). British openly began to rob resources from India including Bengal to help the industrial revolution in Britain. While Britain prospered in wealth, Bengal went through deindustrialization, dire poverty and famines. They took raw materials from Bengal, manufactured the finished products in Britain (enhancing its economy) and brought back the finished products to sell in India (gaining wealth again from the profit).

Kolkata (formerly Calcutta) served as the capital of British controlled territories in India until 1911. For their own existential convenience, western part of Bengal (Kolkata side) underwent rapid industrial growth while the eastern part of Bengal (now Bangladesh) suffered. West side of Bengal not only became more prosperous, it also became the education center for the aspiring youth of Bengal with Kolkata being the only city in Bengal to have a University (University of Calcutta) until 1921. For this reason a significant number of the poets and authors born during British Raj in eastern part of Bengal, moved to Kolkata in their youth.

A section of farsighted Bengali population took advantage of the exposure the British Raj provided to the western world. They embraced modernism in every possible way and took pioneering role in culture, business, science, social reform and many other fields including literature. A few westerners worked hand in hand and shoulder to shoulder with the Bengali population towards these advancements. As Bengal went through renaissance (from nineteenth century through early twentieth century), British rulers realized the need to divide the population in order to sustain. The viceroy of India, George Nathaniel Curzon (Lord Curzon) divided Bengal in 1905 into a Muslim dominated East Bengal and Hindu dominated West Bengal. However, he grossly underestimated the spirit of Bengali speaking population in general, regardless of their religious affiliation. Undivided Bengal was almost as large as France and its population not just resilient but also anchored in its heritage and tradition. Curzon's move gave birth to a severe resistance by the indigenous Bengali population. The British bowed down to the resilience of Bengal and reunited Bengal as one in 1911.

Bengal was divided once again in 1947, during the independence of India when the country was partitioned into two dominions (India and Pakistan) by the British. The political leaders of undivided India were no less culprit for this partition. Muslim dominated East Bengal became part of the newly formed Pakistan, only to be divided again based on language.

The Bengali speaking population of East Bengal demanded Bengali language to be recognized as one of the official languages of Pakistan. As the Pakistani government, led by Muhammad Ali Jinnah denied this petition, the students of Dhaka University, on March 11, 1948 organized a protest rally. Thus, the language movement began. A few years of uncompromising protests and demonstrations eventually culminated into a greater political movement but the government was still unwilling to extend official status to Bengali language. Anticipating escalated tension, the government outlawed public meetings and rallies. Subsequently, the government advised its Bengali speaking population to adopt Arabic script (Arabic script being the scripture of Islam) to write Bengali words. This ridiculous preaching was denounced instantly by the Bengali speaking population and the language movement witnessed an increased fervor. The language movement took a decisive turn as the new governor general of Pakistan, Khawaja Nazimuddin, successor of Muhammad Ali Jinnah, in 1952, echoed the same sentiment professed by his predecessor. Following the speech of Khawaja Nazimuddin, the students and activists of Bengali language movement gathered at the Dhaka University on January 31, 1952 and formed a Central Language Action Committee. An all-out demonstration rally was scheduled for February 21, 1952, however, the government immediately imposed ban over any public gathering. Defying the ban, on February 21, Bengali speaking people from all walks of life began to gather at the premises of the Dhaka University. Police opened fire against the rally and killed Abdus Salam, Rafiq Uddin Ahmed, Abul Barkat and Abdul Jabbar. As soon as the news of firing as well as killings became known to the general population, disorder erupted like volcano all over the city.

Finally, on May 7, 1954, government of Pakistan reworded its constitution and included Bengali along with Urdu as the two official languages of Pakistan. Nonetheless, the Central Language Action Committee decided to observe 21st February of every year as the national Martyr Day and it has been commemorated ever since.

Eventually in 1971, East Bengal (known as East Pakistan since 1956) fought fiercely and earned its independence from Urdu speaking Pakistan. East Pakistan became Bangladesh and the only sovereign nation in the world where Bengali language gained the status of national language.

On November 17, 1999, UNESCO unanimously adopted and declared 21st February to be the International Mother Language Day throughout the world. Each year on 21st February, many events throughout the world are observed towards promoting awareness of linguistic, cultural diversity and multilingualism. Later in 2008 it was recognized by United Nations as well.

Though religion was used by the political leaders to divide the land of Bengal, Bengali speaking people of East Bengal, West Bengal, Tripura and part of Assam as well as all expatriated Bengali speaking souls worldwide, regardless of their religious beliefs, are bound together by the common thread of their mother tongue - Bengali, one of the sweetest languages of the mankind.

Kazi Nazrul Islam (1899 – 1976)

Kazi Nazrul Islam, the national poet of Bangladesh, was born in 1899 in West Bengal, India. The passing away of his father left the family in poverty. Unable to pay the tuition he was compelled to quit school and find work. He became a cook and also worked at a bakery and a tea stall. However, he later returned to school, though never finished his schooling. Right before his school final exam at the age of 18, he left school to join the Indian army and served there for three years.

He began to write poetry, essays, and songs since an early age. However, his 1922 poetry, 'Bidrohee' (Rebel) brought him into limelight and he became known as 'Bidrohee Kobi' or the rebel poet. Nazul was fierce against social injustices, religious barriers between Hindus and Muslims, and gender inequality. As his name spread amongst the masses, British government imprisoned him in 1923 for his revolutionary thoughts and preachings, especially for contents published in his journal called "Dhumketu" (Meteor). But that did not deter him. His writings intensified in jail. A year later, upon his release, Kazi Nazrul Islam jumped into the political movement that was raging against the British rule in India.

Simultaneously, he got engaged in various creative works. He joined His Master's Voice (HMV) gramophone company in 1928 as a music director, composer and lyricist. He wrote and composed hundreds of songs that are known as Nazrulgeeti or songs of Nazrul. Later in 1934, he acted as well as composed music for a movie. In 1939, he joined Calcutta Radio. He became the chief editor of 'Nabayug' (New Era) in 1940.

A strong principled man, Kazi Nazrul Islam walked away from his wedding ceremony in 1921, as a protest against an unreasonable condition placed by the bride's uncle, Ali Akbar Khan, a well-known publisher of the time. Same year during a visit to Coomilla (in Bangladesh) he met Pramila Devi, a Hindu woman, and married her in 1924. Together they had four children. Two of the children died very early. Their two other children Kazi Sabyasachi and Kazi Aniruddha later became famous personalities in their own rights.

In 1945 Kazi Nazrul Islam was awarded with prestigious Jagottaarini medal by the University of Calcutta for his contribution to literature. Later, in 1960, the government of India honored him with one of the highest civilian honors, Padmabhusan. Nonetheless, Nazrul's health had started to deteriorate since 1941. It was alleged, that the British government had slow poisoned him while in prison. But later he was diagnosed with Pick's disease, a neurodegenerative illness. He was treated in mental asylums in India and later in Vienna but eventually all treatments failed and he lost memory and speech completely. He remained unrecovered from his loss of memory and speech for the remaining 35 years of his life.

Kazi Nazrul Islam was a diehard fan and follower of Rabindranath Tagore. He met with Tagore in 1921 for the first time. Kazi Nazrul Islam was highly distressed when Rabindranath Tagore passed away in 1941. It was at that time, he wrote one of his popular poetries 'Rabihaaraa' (Loss of Rabi).

Bangladesh earned its freedom in 1971 and in 1972, Kazi Nazrul Islam was taken to Bangladesh by the Bangladesh government where he eventually passed away in 1976.

The poetry, "God or Ishwar" directs people to journey within. The poet urges the masses to not blindly follow the so-called authorities of God - whether in Hindu or Muslim faith. Instead he inspires people to find God within the self.

God (Ishwar)
Kazi Nazrul Islam

God

Questing god, who are you, search sky and beneath
Who are you roaming in woods and sierra summit?
                              Alas! Sage – Fakir,
Holding gem to your chest, you search Him worldwide!
Creation looks upon you, yet you stand closed eyed,
You meander, Creator seeker, in self-inspection!
Clear your eyes, O greedy-blind! See mirror reflection,
Thou shall see, His aura, in your own appearance.
Do not shudder, Oh valiant, don't fear pundits, –
They're not the almighty's "private secretaries"!
He manifests in populace, in all He's concealed,
Gazing at self, He the Giver is always revealed!
Gems they trade, like a dealer, by Indus-bank –
Gem-maker's path, ask them not, even if by chance.
                              They're gem traders,
Gem-maker they feign to know though appraisers!
Never they drowned for treasure trove to the ocean-floor,
Dive in Truth-sea, instead of treatise, Oh friend explore.

Ishwar

Ke tumi khujichho jagodishey bhaai aakaash paataal jurey
Ke tumi phirichho boney-jangoley, ke tumi paahaar churey?
                              Haay rishi darbesh,
Buker maanikey bukey dhorey tumi khojo taarey desh-desh!
Sristi royechhey tomaa paaney cheye tumi aachho chokh bujey,
Srostaarey khojo – aapanaarey tumi aapani phirichho khujey!
Ichchhaa-andho! Aakhi kholo, dekho darponey nija kaayaa,
Dekhibey, tomaari sob abayabey porechhey taahaar chhaayaa.
Shihari uthhonaa, shaastrobiderey koronaako beer bhoy, –
Taahaaraa khodaar khod "private secretary" to noy!
Sakoler maajhey prokaash taahaar, sakoler maajhey tini,
Aamaarey dekhiyaa aamaar a-dekhaa janmodaataarey chini!
Ratno loiyaa bechaa-kenaa karey bonik sindhu-kooley, –
Ratnaakarer khabor taa boley puchhonaa oder bhuley.
                              Uhaaraa ratno bene,
Ratno chiniyaa mone karey oraa ratnaakareo cheney!
Dubey naai taaraa atal gobheer ratno-sindhutaley,
Shaastro naa ghetey dub daao sakhaa satya sindhu jaley.

Ethereal (Aakaashleenaa)
Jibanananda Dash

Ethereal

Suranjanaa[1], don't go over there,
Don't converse with that fellow;
Come back Suranjana:
To this starry night of sterling glow;

Come back to this realm, to this tidal wave;
To my heart return again;
far to afar – farther away
Don't walk away with the swain.

What is there to confer with him? With him!
Sky hides celestial rondure
Nowadays you are like the loam:
His love grows as verdure.

Suranjanaa,
Today being prairie in your core:
Breeze blows athwart the air –
Empyrean floats beyond the ether.

[1] Suranjanaa or Suranjana is a popular Bengali name for a female. Loosely translated in English it means adequately colorful or beautifully entertaining or many such similar descriptions. 'Su' is a prefix in Bengali and stands for auspicious, beauty, sweet, good etcetera. 'Ranjanaa' or Ranjana on the other hand stands for dyeing, coloring, pleasing or entertaining – depending on its placement.

Aakaashleenaa

Suranjanaa, oikhaaney jeonaako tumi,
Bolonaako kathaa oi jubaker saathey;
Phirey eso Suranjanaa:
Nakshatrer rupali aagun bharaa raatey;

Phirey eso ei maathhey, dhheuye;
Phirey eso hridaye aamaar;
Dur theke durey – aaro durey
Jubaker saathey tumi jeyonaako aar.

Ki kathaa taahaar saathey? Taar saathey!
Aakaasher aaraaley aakaashey
Mrittikaar moto tumi aaj:
Taar prem ghaas hoye aasey.

Suranjanaa,
Tomaar hriday aaj ghaas:
Baataaser opaarey baataas –
Aakaasher opaarey aakaash.

Jibanananda Dash (1899 – 1954)

Jibanananda Dash, originally Jibanananda Dasgupta, was born in 1899 in Barishaal of undivided Bengal. Jibanananda Dash completed his masters' degree in English literature from University of Calcutta in 1921 and subsequently began his professional life as a professor. While still in College, in 1919, he published his first poetry. Subsequently his first collection of poetry "Jharaa Paalak" (Fallen Feathers) was published in 1927.

During his time, Jibanananda Dash was criticized sharply by the literary world and its practitioners. However, Rabindranath Tagore openly appreciated Jibanananda Dash for his poetry "Mrityur aagey" (Before Death), published in 1934. Later Rabindranath Tagore included the same poetry in "Bangla Kaabya Porichoy" (Introduction to Bengali Poetry) compilation, published in 1938. Nonetheless, Jibanananda didn't receive much appreciation during his lifetime. Many of his writings remained unknown until after his demise. One such was "Rupasi Bangla" (Adorable Bengal). He penned it in 1934, however it was not discovered until 1957, two years following his death.

Jibanananda Dash's iconic poetry "Banalataa Sen" was published in 1935 and it was well received in the literary world of Bengal. Later in 1952, 'Banalataa Sen' was published as a collection of poetry by a prominent publisher of the time – Signet Press. The 2nd World War had a profound effect on Jibanananda, which was evident in his collection of poetry titled, "Mahaa Prithibi" (The Vast World), published in 1944. However, the politically instigated division of Bengal, under the British Rule in 1947 created the most impact on him. Along with his family, Jibanananda Dash permanently migrated from his birthplace 'Barishaal' in East Pakistan (now Bangladesh) to Calcutta in West Bengal, India and thus became one of the millions of refugees as part of the largest ever migration of people due to division of a country.

Around 1953-54, Jibanananda Dash began to receive accolades as one of the most prominent poets in the post-Tagore period but he did not live long to enjoy it. "Shresthho Kobitaa" (Superior Poetries), a self-compiled collection of his poetries was published in May 1954 but a tragic accident took his life a few months later in October of the same year. The following year in 1955, "Shresthho Kobitaa" received the prestigious "Saahitya Academy" (Academy of literature) award posthumously.

The translated poetry "Ethereal or Aakaashleenaa" in this book refers to a female named Suranjanaa. Jibanananda Dash wrote many poetries addressing or involving "Suranjanaa." Suranjanaa, loosely translated in English means adequately colorful or colorfully beautiful. Though through majority of his poetry Jibanananda Dash vibrantly expressed his emotions around love, however, his personal love life was not favorable. He loved his cousin Shobhona (his uncle's daughter) deeply but marriage between cousins was not permissible by the society. Under pressure from the family, Jibanananda Dash married Labanyaprabha Gupta, but it turned into a very unpleasant relationship. Eventually it turned so bitter that, his wife visited him but once at the hospital when he was battling for his life for eight days following the accident.

Jibanananda Dash succumbed to his injuries and eventually passed away on October 14, 1954.

Amiya Chakravarty (1901 – 1986)

Dr. Amiya Chakravarty was a profound personality and a scholar in literature. He was born in 1901 in Serampore, (Sreerampur) a suburb of historic importance, near Kolkata, West Bengal. Following his graduation, Amiya Chakravarty joined Rabindranath Tagore's Visva-Bharati as a student in 1921. Subsequently he became a close associate of Tagore and served as Tagore's personal secretary from 1924 to 1933. Chakravarty accompanied Tagore to Europe and America in 1930 and to Iran and Iraq in 1932. In 1933 Amiya Chakravarty moved to Oxford University and earned his D.Phil. in 1937.

Later he returned to India and continued his profession as a professor. He taught English as well as Comparative Oriental Religions and Literature. Following India's independence, he moved to USA in 1948 and continued as an academician at various colleges and universities.

Dr. Chakravarty took active role in India's freedom movement as well. He was closely associated with Mahatma Gandhi (Mohandas Karamchand Gandhi) and took part in the historic Daandi March (salt movement) in 1930, that stretched from Gandhi's Sabarmati Ashram to Daandi (in the state of Gujarat). Later he served as a delegate to the United Nations, representing India.

Throughout his life Dr. Chakravarty wrote many poetries, essays and other articles. His work was published in numerous periodicals and journals in India, England and USA. One of the collection of his verses, 'Gharey Pheraar Din' (Time to return home) received Saahitya Academy award (Academy of literature) in 1963. He also received an award from UNESCO for his collection of poetries, 'Chalo Jaai' (Let's go). Amiya Chakravarty's literature reflected his deep passion in human relationship, humanism, and nature. His book, 'Dynasts and the Post-war Age in Poetry' is a critical work and still used for references and studies.

Amiya Chakravarty edited several English translations of Tagore's works. In his retired life, he moved to Shantiniketan (Shantiniketan is where Rabindranath Tagore established Visva-Bharati University) and remained there till his last breath. He passed away in 1986.

The government of India honored Dr. Amiya Chakravarty with Padmabhushan award in 1970.

In his poetry "Any-Thing or Je-Kono", Amiya Chakravarty brings a woman's romanticized perspective of a family life to life. Her day dreaming of a tranquil, easygoing family of three, where daily chores such as drying clothes in open air is beautifully weaved in this poetry. A picturesque visual of a laid-back lifestyle comes to life through his play of words. It evokes a nostalgia as well as paints a romantic perspective.

Any-Thing (Je-Kono)
Amiya Chakravarty

Any-Thing

Could've been that abode, could've been there
      A singing room to swing the dozy bambino –
      Crimson aubade wallowed bathroom
      Mountain over horizon through open window,
            Mellow sun;
      Clothes drying on backyard line,
      Breezy shade beneath seesawing willow –
          Could've been those
          All mine.

Wide-eyed she dreams passing by
      Roaming yet all these are mine –
      Resting briefly on mat tranquilly
      In the charming noon,
      Books laying open by a cloth-stand,
          Scattered toys,
      Yonder through life with a cozy family.
A phantasm glides at home and abroad
              Could've been all
      Could've been that abode, a triad family.

Je-Kono

Hotey paarto oi ghar, hotey paarto oi
      Ghumono shishukey duliye gaaner ghar –
      Raangaa roddurey lutono snaaner gharey
      Kholaa jaanaalaar aakaashey paahaar,
          Narom surjya;
      Shukochchhey jaamaa baagaaner taarey,
      Jhiri gaachh dolaa haaoyaay chhaayaay –
          Hotey paarto oi
          Sab-i aamaar.

Du-chokh bibhor bhaabchhey pathikaa
      Jetey-jetey tobu sab-i to aamaari –
      Sheetalpaatitey khanobishraam
      Madhur dupurey,
      Aalnaar paashey paataa-kholaa boi,
          Chharaano khelnaa,
      Bharaa-songsaar bukey niye paar haaoyaa.
Deshey bohudeshey chhobi jaagey shudhu
              Hotey paarto oi
      Hotey paarto oi ghar, tiner songsaar.

Train Window (Trener Jaanlaa)
Premendra Mitra

Train Window

Flying greenery, Acacia woods, Verdant lightening
Stirred me. Sweltering two-day train traverse
It didn't avenge. Yet the untamed noontide
Overflow like a stolen bliss of blue-lotus.

Entirety seen only through a window. Withal – all reciprocation,
Vocation, copulation, invocation. Counting days by the window.
Other windows may be extant, search for it though, futile.
Eyes, ears and consciousness built to the ratio of one window.

Yet, if impetus could make me renunciant,
Stagnant could be startled. Afar at horizon unmoving
Stabile hills may budge. Stealing glances in compartment, –
Pointless, fruitless, yet the moment intoxicating.

Over the graveled path, not to protect harvest field,
Or else mill attestant, each one with own station.
Familiar path, familial home, foolproof clock, few blunders.
At times in a flash, a sudden unalike exploration.

Trener Jaanlaa

Uro hariyaaljhaak, baablaabon, sobuj bidyutey
Chhuye gelo. Du'diner galodgharmo trener dhakol
Ushul hoy ni taatey. Tobu jeno duranto dupur
Ekti choraai sukhey neelpadmey karey talomal.

Sob-i jaanlaay dekhaa. Taai diye sob chaaoyaa-paaoyaa,
Jeebikaa, janon, jop. Jaanlaar dhaarey din gonaa.
Aaro Jodi baataayan thaakey, khoja bujhi pandoshram.
Ek jaanlaar-i maapey garaa chokh kaan o chetonaa.

Tobu beg diye Jodi hotey paari kakhono bibaagee,
Achaleraa chamkaay. Bohu dur chakrobaaley sthir
Dhrubo paahaareraa narey. Trener kaamraay chokhaachokhi, –
Maaney nei, nei porinaam, tobu muhoorto modir.

Paathurey prantarey, noy phasoler khet aaglaano,
Kimbaa kaarkhaanaar saakkhee, jaar jaar nijer station.
Chenaa raastaa, chenaa baari, ghori thhik, kichhu bhulchuk.
Kakhono jhalokey shudhu aachomkaa anya anweshan.

Premendra Mitra (1904 – 1988)

Premendra Mitra was born in 1904, in Varanasi, UP, India, though his family home was situated in south 24 Parganas of west Bengal. His father had a travelling job with Indian Railways which gave Premendra the opportunity to travel to many places in India.

In 1920, soon after his High School graduation (matriculation), Premendra Mitra became immersed in literature. His first works were published 3 years later, in 1923 in a prominent literary journal of the time, "Probaasi" (Expatriated). These works received rave reviews from "Kallol" (Uproar) - another significant Journal of the time, catapulting him into the limelight of Bengali literature. Initially Premendra Mitra used his penname for his writings- 'Krittibaas Bhadra'.

Premendra Mitra was a versatile author. In addition to poetry he wrote stories, novels, essays, science fictions and much more. Among the many characters he brought to life through the pages of his stories, two have become iconic amongst his readers- 'Ghanaa da' and 'Mejokartaa.' Ghanaa da is a satirically humorous character, perhaps towards Mitra's sharp criticism of Bengali pseudo-intellectuals. Mejokartaa, on the other hand is a famous ghost hunter.

In his poetry, Premendra Mitra sided with the working class. Adoring beauty, nature and god (in the form of prayer) was the prevalent theme in writings at the time. The field of literature was highly influenced by the likes of Rabindranath Tagore, Bankim Chandra Chattopadhyay, and Satyendranath Dutta. Mitra and many of his contemporaries worked creatively to break out of the prevailing trend and offered a new perspective, style, as well as context. In one of his poetries, Premendra Mitra wrote, 'I am a poet of all the blacksmiths, bell-metal craftsmen, carpenters, day laborers. I am a poet of all the lowly people.'

Mr. Mitra received several awards during his lifetime for his creativity. He was awarded with Sarat Smriti Puraskaar (Sarat Memorial Award) in 1954, Saahitya Academy (Academy of Literature) Award in 1956, Ananda Puraskaar (Ananda Award) in 1973, Nehru Award in 1976. Additionally, he was conferred with prestigious 'Deshikottam' title. He also received Bhubaneswari padak awarded by Shishu Saahitya Parishad (Children's Literary Society) and Haranath Ghosh padak (Haranath Ghosh Award)) conferred by Bangiyo Saahitya Parishad (Bengali Literary Society).

Premendra Mitra also directed a few Bengali movies, among which, 'Haanaabaari' still remains very popular.

Married to Beena Mitra in 1930, he was, by profession, a Bengali professor at City College in north Kolkata. He spent almost his entire adult life in a house at Kalighat, Kolkata. In 1988, at the age of 84, Premendra Mitra passed away in Kolkata.

In his poetry, "Train Window or Trener Jaanlaa", Premendra Mitra uses a window of a train to bring forth the deeper reflections on life. The entire poetry is based on imageries, one sees routinely while occupying a window seat of a train. The window becomes the screen on which the movie of life plays. Drawing parallels as well as contrast between the obvious and the subtle, he creates a surreal impression for the reader and provokes deeper thoughts exploring beyond the routine. The poetry reveals probability of finer intricacies of life, including indulgence in intimacy with life itself, however, doesn't overlook the hard reality of existence. The poetry maintains a subtle balance between reality and aspirations.

Buddhadeb Bosu (1908 – 1974)

Buddhadeb Bosu was one of the most prominent Bengali writers of the 20th century. Though he is referred to as Poet Buddhadeb Bosu, his novels, short stories, plays and essays made him a household name amongst the masses.

Buddhadeb Bosu was born in 1908 in Comilla (now in Bangladesh) of undivided Bengal. His mother passed away within hours of his birth leaving him under the care of his maternal grandparents.

Budhhadeb Bosu became immersed in literature from an early age. At the age of seventeen, he published his first collection of poetries titled, 'Bondeer Bandonaa' (Prayer of the prisoner) followed by his first novel, 'SaDa' at the age of 18. Following his High School graduation, Bosu joined the University of Dhaka to study English and Literature. In 1931, with a Master's degree in English in his hand, the young Bosu moved to Kolkata. Not finding a regular job, he resorted to 'private tuition' for his livelihood. Later he secured a job as a lecturer at Ripon College (Now Surendranath College). In 1956, he pursued the authorities at Jadavpur University to set up the Comparative Literature department, where he remained as a faculty for many years.

Buddhadeb Bosu has been described as a hardworking, disciplined, almost obsessive worker. Work, for him, meant writing. He began his day at 9 in the morning and would work regularly until 10 at night. He has written more than 40 novels and published more than 160 titles during his lifetime. He not only authored a huge volume of novels, essays and poetries, but also introduced foreign literature to Bengal, one of which was the poetries of Charles Baudelaire, the famous French poet. Buddhadeb Bosu was highly fascinated by literature of the western world.

Among his works, 'Tithidore' still remains the most discussed novel and is considered a classic. Though his plays were considered to be highly complex, 'Prathom Partho' and 'Anamni Anganaa' became very popular after his death. Buddhadeb Bosu gained mass popularity when his novel, 'Raat Bharey Bristi' was banned by the government of west Bengal on the charges of obscenity. It depicted a love triangle, where explicit sexuality played a critical role. Eventually the High Court absolved the novel of the charges of obscenity. The novel was later translated in English by Clinton B. Seely with the title 'Rain through the Night'.

Buddhadeb Bosu turned out to be the central personality within the modernist Bengali literary circle of the 20th century. One of his most important contributions to the Bengali literary scene was the establishment of 'Kabitaa'- the flagship poetry magazine in Bengali, which he singlehandedly edited for 25 years. Many poets found this magazine as their stepping-stone into the arena of Bengali literature.

His play Tapaswi O Tarangini earned him the Saahitya Academy Award in 1967. He also received the Rabindra Purashkaar (Rabindra Award) in 1974. Additionally, he was conferred with Padmabhusan title by the government of India in 1970.

In 1934, Buddhadeb Bosu married Pratibha Shome, an accomplished singer and author.

40 years later, in 1974, at the age of 66, Budhhadeb Bosu passed away, leaving behind many unpublished writings that are still finding their place in the pages of literature.

His poetry "Transformation or Roopaantar" reflects a profound philosophical perspective. In this poetry he appreciates all the sensory adorations of life while remaining detached. Life, in this poetry, is lived in wakeful dreams and through pure absolvent moments finds the path to freedom within. The poet embraces death as life as well as the most prominent aspect of existence in this poetry.

Transformation (Roopaantar)
Buddhadeb Bosu

Transformation

My days are livid from tormented toil,
    Nights are sparkled in wakeful dreams.
Awake oh beauty through rub of ore, O white flame,
    Let the corporeal become ethereal, moon – a woman,
        Star in the sky a flower of the soil.
Arise, oh sacred lotus, awake within lotus stalk of life,
    Absolve eon through ungloomy condoning moment,
        Alchemize moment into eon.
Let body be mind, mind be life, let death confluence in life
    Let death transform into body, life, mind.

Roopaantar

Din mor karmer prohaarey paangshu,
    Raatri mor jwalanto jaagroto swapney.
Dhaatur songgharshey jaago hey sundar, shubhro ognishikha,
    Bostupunjo baayu hok, chaad hok naaree,
        Mrittikaay phul hok aakaasher taaraa.
Jaago, hey pobitro padmo, jaago tumi praaner mrinaaley,
    Chirantaney mukti daao khanikaar amlaan khamaay,
        Khonikerey karo chirantan.
Deho hok mon, mon hok praan, praaney hok mrittyur songgom
    Mrittyu hok deho, praan, mon.

Rickshawpaddler (Rickshaawaalaa)
Arun Mitra

Rickshawpaddler

Right here, the rickshaw stops it's wheeling. Waits in front of my dwelling. The man who plies, never fails to show up, even in this bitter winter. As such I recognize him not, for daily his face seems to change. I recognize him by the orbiting wheels.

Impelling his son and wife into darkness he emerges every evening. Which neighborhood he comes from, I know not. Only this much I fathom, he lives across the eerie lights, over the colossal wintery night. Where he lives, matters not. He knows my home, to both of us that matters the most.

Umpteen times I plied in rickshaw, passing by all those streets dashed by wintery tide. During those commutes I witnessed a blaze within him, as if his bone and marrow were on fire. I felt that heat. I feared, intense flapping of his cotton flimsy-shirt would turn my warm clothing into an inferno. But no, each time he was precise, bringing me here, paddling through the eerie lights. Once, his abode seemed very near, yet I felt it not. Even today, commuting me, he will plunge into the wintery night and bring me back safely.

Most likely a day will come he will not arrive. Devoid of his inner flame, frozen into a rock, he will lay abated, wherever. Nonetheless, the wheels of the rickshaw will not be settled in ground. The wheels will orbit again and I would know, the Rickshawpaddler is here, just the way I realize now. For me it is a relief, indeed.

Rickshaawaalaa

Rickshaar chaakaa duto ghurtey ghurtey eikhaantaay esey daaraay. Aamaar baarir saamney apekshaa karey. Je-loktaa chaalaay ekdino taar kaamaai nei, ei bisham thhaandaateo naa. Emnitey taakey dekhey aamaar chenaar kathaa noy, kaaron taar mukhtaa jeno roji badlaay. Chaakaa dutor ghoraa theke chini.

Sondher por chheleboukey andhokaarer modhye thheley diye se beriye parey. Kon mahollaa thekey taa aamaar kaachhey poriskaar noy. Shudhu eituku bujhtey paari, bhuturey aalogulo paar hoye geley ek prokaando je sheeter raat parey taar opaarey se thaakey. Jekhaanei thaakuk kichhu aasey jaay naa. Aamaar baaritaa je taar chena, aamaader du-joner pakkhhey etaai baro kathaa.

Sheeter dhheu je-sob raastaay aachhrey parey sei sob raastaa diye rickshaa chorey aami anekbaar giyechhi. Takhon maanushtaar modhye aagun gongon kortey dekhechhi, mone hoyechhey taar osthimajjaa jwolchhey. Aamaar gaaye sei aach esey legechhey. Taar suteer fotuyaataa takhon tibrobhaabey urtey thaakey ebong aamaar bhoy hoy aamaar garom jaamaakaapor bujhi daau daau korey jwoley uthhbey. Kintu naa, protyekbaari se bhuturey aalogulor modhye diye aamaakey aabaar eikhaaney thhikmoto pouchhey diyechhey. Emonki taar baaritaa je eksamoy khub kaachhaakaachhi ese giyechhilo, a onubhutitaao aar leshmaatro thaakeni. Aajo se aamaakey niye sheeter raater modhye jhaapiye porbey ebong niraapadey aabaar phiriye aanbey.

Khub sambhab kono ekdin se aastey paarbey naa. Bhetorer aaguntaa nibey giye se thaandaay jomey paathor hoye kothaao porey thaakbey. Kintu taa boley rickshaar chaakaa duto to maatitey gerey jaabey naa. Taaraa aabaar ghurbey ebong taai thekey aami bujhbo sei rickshaawaalaa haajir hoyechhey, ekhon jeman bujhi. Etaai aamaar kaachhey ek swasti.

Arun Mitra (1909 – 2000)

Arun Mitra was a poet of the masses. Born in 1909 in Jessore (Bengali pronunciation Jashor), now in Bangladesh. Arun Mitra moved to Kolkata at an early age where he did his schooling. Following completion of higher studies in English literature, Arun Mitra joined the renowned Anandabazar Patrika (A popular Bengali news daily). Later he was awarded a scholarship by the French government that took him to France in 1948. His intense admiration for French literature inspired him to translate several French poets and authors into Bengali. Arun Mitra expressed his gratitude to French literature and attempted to blend French style in his Bengali penmanship. Upon his return to India, Arun Mitra joined Allahabad University in Uttar Pradesh, as a faculty and remained there until retirement.

Arun Mitra edited a literary magazine titled, 'Arani' (Flint). This magazine was known for its anti-fascist stance. As such many activist-writers of the time, found their voice through Arani magazine.

In his poetry, Arun Mitra relentlessly experimented with words to express his deep emotions towards the working-class. "Arun Mitra was constantly frustrated by the inadequacy of words, so he became relentless as he made greater and greater magic with those unruly bits of language—his Bengali words. That's the source of wonderment in his poetry, scattered in more than fifteen books of poetries and eight collections, written over seven decades!" His son, Dr. Ranadhir Mitra wrote, remembering his father. Ranadhir Mitra has elegantly translated a vast number of his father's poetries from its original Bengali into English, which can be found at www.arunmitra.org.

A humanist first, Arun Mitra is quoted as saying, "Thinking about being human has influenced me in another way, I think. It has done away with certain divisions in my mind and in my behavior as well. I do not find a line of demarcation separating educated and uneducated, poet and non-poet, intellectual and non-intellectual. I have never hesitated to embrace as a friend any human being with a heart." Indeed, he was a man of uncompromising principles. The downtrodden of the society found their voice through Arun Mitra's writings.

"Rickshawpaddler or Rickshaawaalaa" is one such poetry written in free verse (almost like a prose). In this poetry, his compassion and understanding for one of the poorest professions and its practitioners in India, shines through. Rickshawpaddler, his life, his tenacity, his endurance takes center stage for the reader. As I read this poetry, I visualized a man-pulled two-wheeler rickshaw, which used to be a common mode of short distance transportation in Kolkata, India. But as I cross-referenced this with his son, I was offered a different visual. According to Dr. Ranadhir Mitra, his father wrote this poetry while residing in Allahabad, India, where a three-wheeler rickshaw (cycle rickshaw), operated by a man paddling it, was also prevalent. "On humanitarian ground, Arun Mitra, never availed a two-wheeler rickshaw pulled by a man", stated his son, Dr. Ranadhir Mitra. Hence the poet was referring to a three-wheeler rickshaw in his poetry. Therefore, though Arun Mitra wrote, "Rickshaar chaakaa duto ghurtey ghurtey eikhaantaay esey daaraay", I applied my liberty to omit the word 'duto' (means two) and transcreated, "Right here, the rickshaw stops it's wheeling", keeping the essence intact. No one can ever be sure, why Arun Mitra chose to use the word "duto" (two) while he wrote about a three-wheeler.

Arun Mitra was married to Shanti Mitra (majumder). Together they built their wondrous world of literature, where they remained by each other's side through thin and thick while compassionately inspiring each other. Shanti Mitra was a short story writer in her own right.

Arun Mitra passed away in 2000, in Kolkata.

Bishnu Dey (1909 – 1982)

Poet Bishnu Dey was born in Kolkata, India in 1909. He completed schooling through Mitra Institution and Sanskrit Collegiate School. Following Bachelor's, he completed Master's degree in English literature and language from the University of Calcutta. He joined Ripon College as a faculty in English literature in 1935. Subsequently he taught at several other colleges throughout his career as a professor in English literature and language.

Like many other poets of the time, Bishnu Dey was also actively associated with "Kallol" (Uproar) magazine and its movements. Along with noted poet Sudhindranath Dutta, he co-edited a literary magazine, "Parichoy" (Acquaint or Introduction or Identity). Later he published a literary magazine on his own – "Nirukto" (Assertion or Enunciation).

Bishnu Dey was a prolific personality. Besides poetry, he also penned essays and prose. He manifested himself through his penmanship in art criticism as well. He was also a cinema critic. His collaboration with renowned artist Jamini Roy, brought forth some of his finest books on arts, authored by him. He was attracted to the literature of the west, especially of T.S. Eliot (Eliot translated many poetries written by Rabindranath Tagore.) Bishnu Dey was also influenced by Marxist philosophy.

His poetry "Staff Reporter or Nijaswa Songbaaddaataa" reflects this influence. Here he talks about the impact of manmade as well as natural calamities on those marginalized by the society. The villages in India are infrastructurally primitive when compared to the cities. The economy, culture, social lifestyle as well as civic amenities differ vastly between villagers and city people. This is evident in this poetry. Besides this stark contrast, the poet incorporates a humanitarian aspect towards the later part of the poetry where he portrays the imagery of a temple with its idols and the benevolence of water (life) for the severely thirsty reporter. The bridge (the reporter) between the civilized urban life (newspaper) and the underprivileged rural life is helpless. The reporter knows that despite the reporting, nothing will really change for the poor except fulfilling his job demands. Both sides of the society remain a mere spectator. Sufferer suffers and the reader of the news remains unmoved, uninvolved onlooker.

To this belief of self and society, Bishnu Dey, following the independence of India, formed "Anti-Fascist Writers' and Artists' Association." He became actively involved in IPTA (Indian People's Theatre Association) founded in 1942. He was also part of Soviet Friendship Association (USSR or Soviet Russia, due to its Communist outlook at the time, was considered to be ideal for Marxism leaning Indian population), and 'Pragatisheel Lekhak Shilpi Sangha' (Progressive Writers' and Artists' Association).

In 1965, Bishnu Dey received the prestigious Sahitya Academy Award (Academy of Literature Award). His book, Smriti Swatwaa Bhabisyat (Past Present Future) received the highest literary award in India, Gyanpeethh (Receptacle of Knowledge). Additionally, Bishnu Dey received many other awards for his literary contribution such as the Nehru Award and the Soviet Land Award.

Bishnu Dey was married to Pranati Dey. The poet passed away in 1982 in Kolkata (Calcutta).

Staff Reporter (Nijaswa Songbaaddaataa)
Bishnu Dey

Staff Reporter

I work for a newspaper.
Sparsity of food, swarming refugees from East Bengal,
Fiercely troubled Bengal; hence report was sought.
Wearied I travelled to sweltering camps, sheltering-slums
Village to village, scorching fields, sultry homeland
Now-a-days, a perpetual yearly famine, I find.
Scorching sun atop, ruptured fields on earth
Knee-high dust at places,
No trace of water, dazed faces of people,
Deep rancor, disbelief, dying hope of dispossessed.

I profess: Gentle in appearance, but just a reporter,
Never asked to be voted, never divided motherland impudently,
My avarice for privileged power pleasure
Didn't origin misfortune for millions.
Merely a reporter, a gentleman, that's all
Actually, as helpless, enslaved, sun parched,
Though not starved, yet a forlorn forsaken soul of history,
Absolute bereft, bitter, burnt, pristine.
I declined local babu's jeep, new motor ride of the leader,
Availing public bus, I heed: Embracing local praxis, I walk.

I walked, journeyed from village to village
Entire district arid indigent, starvation blazed all.
Western desert like heat. I recall even today,
The ferocity I felt. Monsoon rain doesn't downpour anymore.
Predictable evenings of nor'-wester are here no more.

I remember one time, dying coal in the village clay-oven,
Fire burning the sky, fire flowing on ground.
East-village bound, I wasn't a sub-judge or an official or a nawab,
Early morning the journey began. What a barren land! Miles upon miles
As if thousands of killers, over several centuries
Murdered the earth by ripping it apart,
Mango-rose apple-jackfruit-peepul nothing in sight, pond-well-
Canal-strait, dried stream none for respite.
Just bloodless blanch sunshine.
Distressed I was in thirst. I still remember, at once
On my left, abaft Kantadanga[1], a temple came in sight
Humble, crumbling, lifeless. I approached.
Hoping for water, seeking shield to veil thirst n hunger
Heedlessly I peeked.

Looking back, I still recall that absolute darkness,
Mother's unctuous black eyes in wondrous tender shade,
Soothing my sight body soul O! The comfort of black.
My sight unclouded, I glimpsed the nude idol couple
Unattired; touchstone made indigenous Radha and Ghanashyam,[2]
No glory of worship, yet a redolence reigned
Heavenly coitus stone, from where it's fragrance flowed?
Abaft the alter, revealed on the black-stoned indent, zoetic
A few lonely magnolias braving the negligence
Immortal yellow hued glorious in blossom and grace.
And in the left corner unearthed a lidded earthen pitcher full of water.

[1]'Kantadanga' is a name of a locality. Loosely translated in English it means land of thorn.

[2]Ghanashyam is another name of lord Krishna. Loosely translated it means densely Black. 'Ghana' is thick and 'Shyam' means dark blue, dark green and jet black. Radha is Krishna's consort.

Nijaswa Songbaaddaataa

Khaborer kaagojer kaaj.
Khaadyaabhaab, purbobangotyagee bhir,
Banglaay samosyaa ugro, taai cheyechhey report.
Ghuri tiktotaay dagdho campey, chhaauni-bostitey
Graamey graamey, poraa maathhey pora deshey
Jekhaaney ekaaley, mone hoy chirokaal baarshik aakaal.
Maathaay prachando roudro, paaye maati kothaao chouchir
Kothaao baa hatu dhulo,
Jal nei, maanusher chokhey mukhey jal nei,
Shudhu ghrinaa, abishwaas, deerghokaal bonchiter sandeho songshoy.

Bojhaai: Dekhtey bhadro ei maatro, kintu shudhu reporter,
Kakhono niyini vote, desh swaadheenmostitey
Bhaangi ni, kayek koti maanusher durbhaagaa kapaaley
Haani ni raajyer lobh khamotaar keraamatey sukhey.
Shudhumaatro reporter, bhadrolok eimaatro,
Aasoley ederi moto asohaay, paraadheen, roudrey poraa,
Hoyto pettaa bharey, athocho hridoy itihaasey asohaay boli,
Ekebaarey nihsambol, tikto, pora, khaati.
Chherey diyi sthaaniyo babur jeep murubbir notun motor,
Mafosswalee bus dhori, bhaabi: Jekhaaney jemon riti, haati.

Haati, ei graam theke jaai oi graamey
Nirjalaa abhaab saaraataa jelaay, sarbotroi ek upobaasee jwaalaa.
Edikey garom praay poshchimaa morur. Aajo jodi bhaabi,
Jwaalaa taar gaaye laagey. Aamaader aashaareo bristi koi naamey.
Aamaader uthhey gechhey boishaakhir boikaaleer paalaa.

Mone parey ekdin, se-graamey ununey
Aagun nibanto, aagun aakaashey tolaa, aagun maatitey dhhaalaa.
Jete habey pubgraamey, sadraalaa noi, noi naayeb nabaab,
Sutoraang sakaalei jaatraarambho. Se ki Maathh! Mile mile
Anek shataabdee dhorey haajaar haajaar khuney
Prithibikey chhirey chhirey merey gechhey jeno,
Aam-jaam-kaathhaal-pipul kichhu nei, deeghi-kuyaa-
Khaal-bil majaanodi kichhu nei.
Shudhu neerakto shwetaango roudro.
Trishnaar aabegey chokh faatey. Se samoye, aajo mone parey,
Baaye kaataadaangaar aaraaley hathhaat mondir ek dekhaa jaay
Chhoto, bhaangaa, janoheen. Sedikei choli.
Jaler aashaay khudhaa aar pipaasaay chhaayaar aashaay
Naa bhebei uki diyi.

Mone parey aajo mone parey sei sarbongsaho andhokaar,
Aashcharjya komol chhaayaa maayer chokher snigdho andhokaar,
Chokh deho hridoy juraano aahaa kaalor aaraam.
Chokher jeeban pherey, dekhi nagno jugal bigraho
Beshbhusaaheen; shudhu kosthhipaathorer deshee Radha aar
Ghanashyam, Nei pujaar gourab, athocho kothaay gandho
Aarotir shringaarer paathorey stombhito kothaay sourav?
Bedeer pichaney dekhi beche aachhey kaalo paathorer dhaapey
Him andhokaarey eka kaektaa kaathhchaapaa
Mrityuheen gorochanaa baahaarer gandher prataapey.
Aar ba-diker koney dekhi sajol maatir ekti kolsi mukhchaapaa.

Sickle (Kaastey)
Dinesh Das

Sickle

Let the bayonet be sharper
Sharpen the sickle my friend,
Let bullet and bomb be mightier
Whet the sickle O my friend!

Arced white slice of the moon
Did you find much lovable?
This centurial is not of moon,
Lune of the epoch is sickle!

Whoever heaped the whole world
With iron and steel yesteryears,
Pecking between the cannons
Imploded themselves in splinters.

World of iron pulverized
Into ocean of your blood
Erodes, rotting in the soil,
Era rising from land's toil.

Dirt thickens over the edge
Witness O my comrade!
Have you whetted the sickle yet?
Soil ally is sickle blade!

Kaastey

Bayonet hok jato dhaaraalo
Kaasteytaa shaan diyo bondhu,
Shell aar bom hok bhaaraalo
Kaasteytaa shaan diyo bondhu!

Baakaano chaader saadaa phaaliti
Tumi bujhi khub bhaalobaastey?
Chaader shatok aaj nahey to,
A-jooger chaad holo kaastey!

Lohaa aar ispaatey duniyaa
Jaaraa kaal korechhilo purno,
Kaamaaney kaamaaney thhokaathhukitey
Nijeraai churnobichurno.

Churno a louher prithibi
Tomaader raktosomudrey
Khoyito golito hoy maatitey,
Maatir – maatir joog oordhey.

Digantey mrittikaa ghanaaye
Aasey oi, cheye dekho bondhu!
Kaasteytaa rekhechho ki shaanaaye?
A-maatir kaasteytaa bondhu!

Dinesh Das (1913 – 1985)

Dinesh Das, a distinguished Bengali poet, was born in 1913 in Alipore, 24 Parganas district (now Kolkata district), India. Around the age of 15, Dinesh Das became drawn to politics. In ninth grade, he became a member of the underground revolutionary movement supporting India's independence from the British. Subsequently he associated himself with Mohandas Karamchand Gandhi's Satyagraha (non-violent) movement. Satyagraha is a term coined by Gandhiji, probably in or around 1906, while he was practicing as a lawyer in South Africa. It was developed to resist the authorities in South Africa, against a discriminatory action taken by them against the Indian and Chinese population residing there. Upon his return to India in 1915, Gandhiji advanced this concept of non-violent movement against the British government in India. Later this concept was adopted by Martin Luther King, Jr. and James Luther Bevel during the Civil Rights Movement in the USA.

Nonetheless, Dinesh Das's involvement in active politics caused obstacles in his schooling. He somehow managed to complete matriculation (High School) in 1930. Later he studied at South Suburban College (Now Ashutosh College) and also at Scottish Church College.

In 1934, while still in college, his first poetry "Sraaboney" (During Monsoon) was published in one of the most prominent commercial literary magazine, 'Desh' (It is still a leading fortnightly literary magazine, allegorically referred to as the 'New Yorker' of Bengal). However, he dropped out of college due to his passion in politics and literature. In 1935, he found a job at a Tea Estate in Kurseong, (in north West Bengal) and moved there. He engrossed himself in self-study, which soon led to disillusionment about Gandhiji and his movement. Instead he found confidence in Marxism.

The following year, in 1936, Dinesh Das returned to Kolkata (Calcutta) and in 1937 penned "Kaastey" (Sickle), perhaps his most popular poetry, ever. This poetry became almost like an anthem for the Marxist-Leninist activists in West Bengal during the sixties and the seventies. It is still a very popular poetry in general.

Kaastey or sickle can be found on several national and communist affiliated party flags throughout the world, including Russia, China, Albania, Algeria, Serbia, Ireland, Turkey, Estonia, Kyrgyzstan, Latvia, Libya, Lithuania, Czechoslovakia, Germany, Nepal, Thailand, South Africa and many more. All flags of the communist parties in India consist of a sickle in their signage or symbol. Sickle is an instrument for the peasants in India (elsewhere as well) where through their manual labor they produce crop for the general population, yet remain as one of the most neglected, starved, and impoverished class of people. In this poetry, "Sickle or Kaastey" Dinesh Das eloquently preaches them to keep their sickles sharpened and not to fear the cannons and bombs and bayonets of the ruling class. He inspires the peasants and their supporters to stand up against all injustices towards them, being armed with their sickles. Sickle in this poetry represents an allegorical significance towards courage and resilience of the oppressed. In contrast of romanticism of a moon, he asks people to embrace reality of revolution. He preaches a sharp essence of communism in this poetry.

Communist party in India was formed in 1925, however, was highly disorganized. Later it came into prominence through sacrifices and leaderships of many. Historically, the communist movement fractionized over the years and lost its mass appeal. However, it is still a significant political power especially in the states of West Bengal, Tripura, Kerala, Andhra Pradesh, Tamilnadu and Punjab. A fraction of the Communist Party of India, Communist Party of India (Marxist) or CPI(M) led coalition of other leftist parties, democratically governed the state of West Bengal from 1977 till 2011.

Poet Dinesh Das remained a sympathizer of communist belief and wrote many more poetries to uplift its philosophy and vision.

He passed away in 1985 in Kolkata (Calcutta).

Saroj Dutta (1915 – 1971)

Saroj Dutta, known as comrade SD, primarily a political intellect, was born in a family of landlords in 1914 in Jessore (now in Bangladesh), India. Following his schooling at Victoria Collegiate School, he moved to Kolkata (Calcutta) and completed Master's degree in English from University of Calcutta in 1938. However, he gave up his privileged life to uphold the rights and privileges of the downtrodden.

In 1940 he joined one of the leading English dailies of the time, Amrita Bazar Patrika and later became the chief editor of the Daily, however, was ousted from the newspaper in 1949 due to his involvement with the Communist Party of India. Following the Indo-China war (Sino-Indian war) in 1960s, he was briefly imprisoned due to his pro-China (Maoist) outlook. Historically, it has been noticed, that the government of any non-communist country fears the strength of communism and instead of engaging in political solution utilizes the power vested in them against the communist believers to uproot them completely. In case of Saroj Dutta, the same was explicitly visible.

As the Communist Party of India (Marxist) or CPI(M) fractioned out of the CPI in 1964, Saroj Dutta leaned towards CPI(M) for his ideological belief. The same year, he became the joint editor of 'Swaadhinataa" (Freedom or Independence), the newspaper of the party.

Within a few years, CPI(M) changed its position and decided to enter the election fray. The communist party once again divided based on ideological differences, since a section didn't believe in parliamentarian process. Around 1967, a movement began to draw attention throughout the state. It originated in a small village called Naxalbari, situated in Darjeeling district in West Bengal. Led by peasant leader Charu Majumdar (1918 – 1972), Naxalbari movement gave birth to CPI(ML) or Communist Party of India (Marxist-Leninist) in 1969. Saroj Dutta was a founding member of CPI(ML). But CPI(ML) was later outlawed in 1970 due to its expressed political ideologies. The entire party continued to operate from underground creating massive impact. Fearing its prominence, the government soon adopted to atrocious measures to eradicate it. Mercilessly, the government machineries, especially the police, murdered hundreds of thousands of people between 1969 and 1972. It was no less than Nazi torture or any genocide.

On August 4, 1971, around midnight the police arrested Saroj Dutta from a hideout. At the time Saroj Dutta was the editor of the journal of CPI(ML), The Liberation. The next morning during wee hours, police took Saroj Dutta to the infamous 'Maidan' (A vast open field) of Calcutta and released him. As he began to walk away from the prison van, police shot and killed him from behind. Later, in their propaganda, police declared, Saroj Dutta attempted to escape from police custody and was shot.

Following Saroj Dutta's murder, Charu Majumdar quoted Mao Tse-Tung or Mao Zedong, "It is not hard for one to do a bit of good. What is hard is to do good all one's life and never do anything bad, to act consistently in the interest of the broad masses, the young people and the revolution, and to engage in arduous struggle for decades on end. That is the hardest thing of all!" Charu Majumdar added: "Comrade Saroj Dutta was such a comrade."

The following year, in 1972, Charu Majumdar, too was tortured to death by the police in his prison cell within ten days following his arrest and without any trial.

Translating Roma Rolland's 'I Will Not Rest', Saroj Dutta once wrote, "…Without a doubt, Rolland died in consequence of the torture he suffered at the Nazi concentration camp. This is why his death makes us more proud than aggrieved." Quoting this translation, Saroj Dutta's wife, Bela Dutta (herself an active cadre of the party) wrote, "…we too, along with all our country people, feel proud of Saroj babu."

His poetry in this collection, "Fancied Revolution of Middle-class or Madhyabitter Biplab-Bilaas" takes aim at the apathy of the middle-class. The poet simply mocks the opportunist and self-doubting middle-class population, who envision a revolution yet never take steps towards fulfilling it, chiefly due to their indecisiveness under the spell of perceived fear.

Fancied Revolution of Middle-Class
(Madhyabitter Biplab-Bilaas)
Saroj Dutta

Fancied Revolution of Middle-Class

Inferno of midday summer makes me swoon,
Craving water, yearning shade, I await monsoon,
Once the Nor'-wester dumps all I prayed,
Inside my hut, dreading – I still am dismayed.

Madhyabitter Biplab-Bilaas

Boishaakher Madhyadiney agnidaahey murchhaatur aami,
Chaahi jal, chaahi chhaayaa, chaahi bristidhaaraa,
Sakoli aanibey jabey mahaamegh kaalboishaakhir,
Paataar kutirey aami utkanthhaay habo dishaahaaraa.

Flowers of Pebbles (Paathorer Phool)
Subhash Mukhopadhyay

Flowers of Pebbles

1

Forsake the flowers,
It's flailing me.

Wreaths
Mound to be mountain,
Flowers
Pile to be pebbles.

Pull off the pebbles,
It's pinching me.

Here and now
Ripped tough gent, no more I am.
Sun-bathe, water, nor a breeze –
Onto this frame
Nothing is bearable now.

Consider,
Mother's tender child, I am now –
Simply, I may wither.

Fronting my journey
I took off at the pristine sunup
Parading, the sun is starting to set.
En route
Why hold me up?

Prolonged impasse passes
Cart is sluggishly wheeling now.
At street-corner
The flower shop is swarmed.
Which Moira fortuned him this morning?

2

Precisely what I speculated
It replicated exact, indeed.
The incense sticks, ascetic resin, garlands, the procession –
Once the night is over
        Ennobling flock will gather!
(Except for the flower-hugging-paper-
Name-tags)
All in all, everything matched precisely.

Softened Sentiments around –
Perfect timing is this.
If the arm outstretched to beg
Cremation tariff will be set.

In a corner, clad in a torn shirt
Dried eyed
grating his teeth
My lad
Sits – formed as wad.

My naïve heir,
Shame shame, is this your valor?
Winter has just begun
How can we concede to tremor?

Forsake the flowers,
It's flailing me,
Wreaths
Mound to be mountain,
Flowers
Pile to be pebbles.

Pull off the pebbles,
It's pinching me.

3

Men compel flowers
To lie a great deal –
Thus, flowers don't enchant me ever.
Rather, I prefer
Floret of fire –
Which can never become somebody's mask.

Things would turn out exactly this way
I knew.
Billowing bubbles of adoration would overflow someday
This I realized.
In whichever chest
In whatever receptacles I may garner
All my affections –
Will remain just as mine.

I witnessed through sleepless nights
How long does it take – how the dawn cracks;
My whole day was spent
In deciphering the mystery of darkness.
Not for a day, not even for a moment
I paused.
I wrung juice out of life and
Stored in pitchers of my heart –
Today it outthrusted.

No.
I am not appeased by mere talks anymore,
Where all the talks emanate from,
Where they culminate –
To that origination of words,
Conclusively in that,
Water-Earth-Air
I wish to meld myself.

Alter the shoulders[1].
Now
May the heaped wood acquire me.
May the delightful floret of fire
Help me heal
All the hurts bestowed by flowers.

---

[1] A dead body is typically laid on a florally decorated cot. The cot is carried over the shoulders of family members, neighbors and friends of the family in a procession on the way to a crematorium. Dead body is also transported by hearse vehicles, especially for affluent and for people of repute. In this poetry, the poet applied both portrayals.

Paathorer Phool

1

Phoolgulo soriye naao,
Aamaar laagchhey.

Maalaa
Jomey jomey paahaar hoy,
Phool
Jomtey jomtey paathor.

Paathortaa soriye naao,
Aamaar laagchhey.

Ekhon aar
Aami sei dashaashoi jowaan noi.
Rod naa, jal naa, haaowaa naa –
A shorirey aar
Kichhui soy naa.

Mone rekho,
Ekhon aami maa-r aadurey chhele –
Ektutei goley jaabo.

Jaabo boley
Se ikon sakaaley beriyechhi
Uthhtey uthhtey sondhyey holo.
Raastaay
Aar keno aamaay daar karaao?

Anekkhon themey thaakaar por
Gaari ekhon dhhikiye dhhikiye cholechhey.
Morey
Phooler dokaaney bhir.
Loktaa aaj kaar mukh dekhey uthhechhilo?

2

Thhik jaa bhebechhilaam
Hubohu miley gelo.
Sei dhoop, sei dhuno, sei maalaa, sei michhil –
Raat pohaaley
        Sabha-tabhaao habey!
(Ekmaatro phooler-galaa-jaraano-kaagojey lekhaa
Naamgulo baadey)
Samastoi hubohu miley gelo.

Mongulo ekhon narom –
Ebong ei hochchhey samoy.
Haat ektu baaraatey paarlei
Ghaat kharochtaa uthhey aasbey.

Ekkoney chheraa jaamaa porey
Shukno chokhey
Daatey daat diye
Chheletaa aamaar
Putuli paakiye bosey.

Bokaa chhele aamaar,
Chhi chhi, ei tui beerpurush?
Sheeter to sabey shuru –
Ekhoni ki kaapley aamaader chaley?

Phoolgulo soriye naao,
Aamaar laagchhey,
Maalaa
Jomey jomey paahaar hoy
Phool
Jomtey jomtey paathor.

Paathortaa soriye naao,
Aamaar laagchhey.

3

Phoolke diye
Maanush baro beshi mithye balaay bolei
Phooler opor konodin-i aamaar taan nei.
Taar cheye aamaar pachhondo
Aaguner phoolki –
Jaa diye konodin kaaro mukhosh hoy naa.

Thhik emontaai je habey,
Aami jaantaam.
Bhaalobaasaar phenaagulo ekdin uthley uthhbey
A aami jaantaam.
Je-buker
Je-aadhaarei bhorey raakhi naa keno
Bhaalobaasaagulo aamaar –
Aamaar-i thaakbey.

Raater por raat aami jegey thekey dekhechhi
Katokkhoney kibhaabey sakaal hoy;
Aamaar dinomaan gechhe
Andhokaarer rahasya bhed kortey.
Aami ek din, ek muhurter janyeo
Thaami ni.
Jeeban thekey ros ningrey niye
Buker ghatey ghatey aami dhheley rekhechhilaam –
Aaj taa uthley uthhlo.

Naa.
Aami aar shudhu kathaay tusto noi,
Jekhaan thekey samosto kathaa uthhey aasey,
Jekhaaney jaay –
Kathaar sei utsey,
Naamer sei porinaamey,
Jal-maati-haaowaay
Aami nijekey mishiye ditey chaai.

Kaadh badol karo.
Ebaar
Stupaakaar kaathh aamaakey nik.
Aaguner ekti ramaniyo phoolki
Aamaakey phooler samosto byatha
Bhuliye dik.

Subhash Mukhopadhyay (1919 – 2003)

Subhash Mukhopadhyay, popularly known as the Padaatik kobi or the foot-soldier poet, was born in 1919 in Krishnanagar (Nadia district), West Bengal. He attained 'Padaatik Kobi' nickname due to his first collection of poetries titled, 'Padaatik', published in 1940 while he was still a student. This collection marked a prominent departure from 'Kallol' (Uproar) era style of writing and introduced a fresh phase in Bengali post-modern poetry. The collection was overwhelmingly well received by the poetry-lovers and placed him in prominence.

A brilliant student, Subhash Mukhopadhyay, completed his Bachelor's degree with honors in philosophy, in 1941. He studied at Scottish Church College in north Kolkata (Calcutta).

Departing from ornamental riddle-like verse formation, Subhash Mukhopadhyay wrote in straight-forward and easily understandable format. His poetries were non-romantic and primarily dealt with social commitments of the time. 1940s was a decade dominated by World War II, a manmade famine that plagued the entire state of Bengal, division of India as well as partition of the state of Bengal. All these events and their effects were documented in Subhash Mukhopadhyay's poetry and writings. Since an early age, Subhash Mukhopadhyay was politically inclined and while in college, formally joined the student wing of Communist Party of India. He remained an active worker of the party for many years, though eventually, much later in life, became disillusioned and withdrawn. At one-point Subhash Mukhopadhyay was briefly imprisoned for his political activities and beliefs as well as for its direct reflection in his writing.

His flamboyancy not only reigned during the 50s and 60s, but was also adopted and followed by many young poets of the time. Though he became an institution in himself, a gradual decline in his fierceness was noticeable from 70s onwards. Instead of direct political or sociological themes, he began to write more on self-introspections and personal emotions as well as on aesthetical aspects of life. His poetries began to reflect more philosophical analysis than anything else. Many characterized this departure from politics as a compromise with the authority of government.

In addition to poetry, Subhash Mukhopadhyay also wrote novels, essays, travelogues and translated poetries. He also wrote children rhymes and stories. Along with Satyajit Ray, he edited the popular children's magazine, 'Sandesh.' (Sandesh means news, message, report or command. It is also a popular Bengali sweetmeat.) Subhash Mukhopadhyay has been translated in many Indian and foreign languages. Library of Congress has nearly forty titles of Subhash Mukhopadhyay.

Subhash Mukhopadhyay received numerous awards in his lifetime. In 1964, he received the Saahitya Academy Award (Academy of Literature Award) followed by Afro-Asian Lotus Prize in 1977, Kumaran Asan Award in 1982, Mirzo Tursun Zade Prize in 1982, Ananda Puraskar (Award of Ananadabazar Group, the leading Bengali daily) in 1991 and Gyanpeethh (Receptacle of Knowledge) Award in 1991. He was also conferred with the prestigious 'Deshikottam' title by Visva-Bharati University and Padmabhusan by the government of India.

In his poetry, "Flowers of Pebbles or Paathorer Phool" Subhash Mukhopadhyay narrates a deceased body's last journey towards the crematorium (funeral home) who may have been a prominent personality yet financially unwell. The poetry accounts sentimental reflections from the perspective of the deceased. His disillusionments are vividly expressed and his complaints are surfaced. Satirical in nature, in this poetry, Subhash Mukhopadhyay also condemns the vanity and fanfare demonstrated by the fans and followers, especially through the usage of flower. He finds pretentious solidarity in fake mourning and feels pain from every petal and every bouquet of flowers as those are rested over his dead body as a gesture of affection, respect and admiration. The deceased wish to rise in truth as the lie from every flower appears to be a torture of pebbles.

Subhash Mukhopadhyay married Gita Bandyopadhyay (also an author and political activist) in 1951. Together, they adopted four children – three daughters followed by a son. Subhash Mukhopadhyay passed away in Kolkata at the age of 84 in 2003.

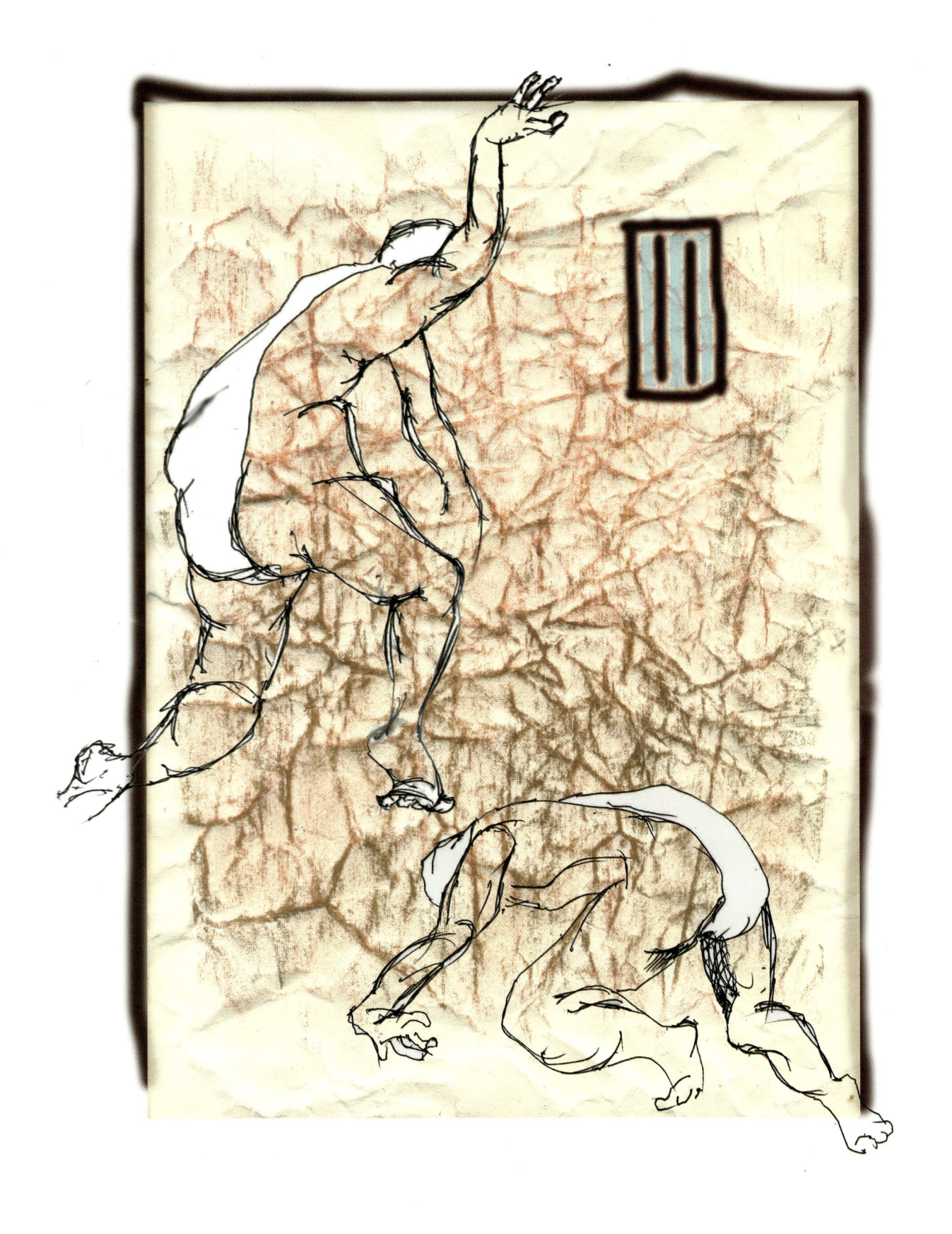

Motherland Now (Janmobhumi Aaj)
Birendra Chattopadhyay

Motherland Now

For once turn your sight to the soil
Once towards humans.

Night is not over yet;
Darkness still lays on your chest
Much like the hardened stone, you are unable to breathe.
A frightening black sky looms atop
Still sitting with its tiger like paws.
Somehow you must remove that rock
And declare calmly to the menacing sky
You are not afraid.

Soil is bound to be ablaze
If nescient in harvest you are
Mantra for monsoon if you forget
Arid your homeland becomes.
Song, if bipeds unable to croon
When holocaust advents, turn mute and blind.
Turn your sight to the soil, it is awaiting,
Take the hand of mankind, they're yearning to tell something.

Janmobhumi Aaj

Ekbaar maatir dikey taakaao
Ekbaar maanusher dikey.

Ekhono raat shesh hoy ni;
Andhokaar ekhono tomaar buker opor
Kothhin paathorer moto, tumi nihshwaas nitey paarchho naa.
Maathaar opor ektaa bhoyongkar kaalo aakaash
Ekhono baagher moto thaabaa uchiye bosey aachhey.
Tumi jebhaabey paaro ei paathortaakey soriye daao
Aar aakaasher bhoyongkarke shaanto galaay ei kathaataa jaaniye daao
Tumi bhoy paao ni.

Maatito aaguner moto habei
Jodi tumi phasol phalaatey naa jaano
Jodi tumi brishti aanaar montro bhuley jaao
Tomaar swadesh taaholey morubhoomi.
Je maanush gaan gaaitey jaaney naa
Jakhon proloy aasey, se bobaa o andho hoye jaay.
Tumi maatir dikey taakaao, se protikshaa korchhey,
Tumi maanusher haat dharo, se kichhu boltey chaay.

Birendra Chattopadhyay (1920 – 1985)

Poet Birendra Chattopadhyay was born in 1920 in Bikarmpur, Dhaka. (Dacca as distortedly pronounced by the British, however, remained as the official spelling for many years.) India was one country back then consisting of, what is now known as India, Bangladesh and Pakistan. Dhaka is the capital of present day Bangladesh.

Like many other poets, Birendra Chattopadhyay also moved to Kolkata at an early age and completed his higher studies from Rippon College. Since he led his entire life as a commoner, his life has not been documented publicly to a great extent. However, a translated collection of his poetries by Robert Hampson and Sibani Raychaudhuri (illustration by Bijan Chaudhury) published by Thema Books, elaborately discusses his poetics as well as about his poetries.

Younger to Birendra Chattopadhyay, though contemporary, poet Sankha Ghosh described him, "In every sense, Bengal's foremost poet of protest." Indeed, Birendra Chattopadhyay protested through nearly each of his poetries. He protested against any and all social injustices, especially the ones of political origination. A firm believer in Marxist philosophy, Birendra Chattopadhyay was an active member of the Communist Party. He led a very strong-willed and principled life till his last day. For that, during the latter part of his life, he disassociated himself from the communist party though remained faithful to his political beliefs. Leadership of communist parties disillusioned many throughout the world. West Bengal was no different. It is perhaps not the theory and philosophy of communism that are flawed, however, the practitioners are human beings who also grow from within the culture of feudalism and capitalism. To believe in a philosophy is one thing, to disassociate from flawed culture is another. Nonetheless, there are people like poet Birendra Chattopadhyay, who consciously gave up popular and prevailing way of life as they truthfully embraced what was right.

Through and through anti-establishment, poet Birendra Chattopadhyay never allowed his writings to be published in any commercially established publication. It was only in his death bed (he died from cancer), following sincere request by a big-name publishing house, he permitted two of his poetries for publishing in that magazine. All his poetries otherwise were published in little-magazines. Anti-establishment in nature, Bengal is known for its little-magazine movement. These magazines are only little in publication size since they don't receive much of advertisement or other financial patronage and sustain primarily on individual monitory contributions. However, often these magazines bring out the best of literature as has been happening traditionally since the Bengal Renaissance. Birendra Chattopadhyay's poignant writings published in various little-magazines, made him a poet of the commoners. He remained with them, he remained for them, forever.

Birendra Chattopadhyay didn't write for money. He wrote because he believed in writing. He wrote because someone needed to be the voice of the oppressed. He wrote because India's independence didn't necessarily free its population. It only created opportunities for the leaders for their personal growth and prosperity. From the heinous British rule to the self-governing Indian democracy, nothing really reversed the downgrading trend of general life. Poor continued to be poorer and the rich richer. Calculated failure of governing bred the need of people like Birendra Chattopadhyay to stand up. And he didn't fail to stand up for the masses. He was imprisoned for this. Yet didn't retract.

His poetry, "Motherland Now or Janmobhumi Aaj" is one such poetry where he passionately converses with the country and urges her to be courageous, conscientious and compassionate for her people. Birendra Chattopadhyay wrote this poetry in 1970, when West Bengal was undergoing the peak of Naxalbari movement, led by Communist Party of India (Marxist-Leninist). It was around then as well, when the state government led oppression under the leadership of chief minister Siddhartha Shankar Ray of Congress Party, rose to its height.

A positive rôle model for all, poet Birendra Chattopadhyay passed away in Kolkata in 1985.

Nirendranath Chakraborty (1924 –)

Poet Nirendranath Chakraborty was born in 1924. He has authored over 65 books, but not all of them are poetry books. In addition to poetry Nirendranath Charaborty also writes rhymes and stories for juveniles, novels, essays and travelogues.

Following his graduation from St. Paul's College in Kolkata, Nirendranath Chakraborty began his work life as a journalist. He worked for several daily newspapers of the time. He emerged as a poet in the 1950s. The finer aspects of human mind and its inner senses including conflicts, come to life through his poetries. As much as Jibanananda Dash painted the rural Bengal in his poetries, Nirendranath Chakraborty uncovered the urban life with equal eloquence through his poetries.

"Fourth Child or Choturtho Santaan" is one such poetry. Indian democracy went through a severe crisis in the 1970s. Indian National Congress led by Indira Gandhi was the ruling party in the Indian parliament and declared a state of emergency in 1977. Under the state of emergency, a government is empowered to take any measures or steps towards governing the country. Among many other undemocratic policies, 'Nasbandi' was also forcefully implemented throughout the country. 'Nasbandi' is a Hindi word where 'Nas' means vein and 'Bandi' means binding. Government health workers were strictly instructed to apply sterilization upon anyone with two or more children. It created a tremendous uproar within the population. Once the state of emergency was lifted and as the country entered the next general election, the electorates mandated a humiliating defeat for the Indian National Congress. It is alleged, Indira Gandhi's son, Sanjay Gandhi unscrupulously ordered mass vasectomy. No one was spared by him, if they failed its implementation.

It was at that time, poet Nirendranath Chakraborty wrote this poetry, Fourth Child. In a very straightforward manner, the poet brings out agony, pain and subsequent protest of a fourth child within an urban setting. (This poetry has a special significance for me personally. I am a fourth child as well. Issues raised and situation described in this poetry are highly relatable to me, I must admit. I cannot deny undergoing similar questions and issues internally within myself from time to time though I had very loving parents who unfortunately passed away when I was young. My sincerest gratitude to poet Nirendranath Chakraborty for allowing me to borrow the title of the poetry as the title of this collection. This subject is very close to my heart). Though the state of emergency ended and the dominance of the Gandhi family has faded, however, the professed culture has been widely adopted by the population. In the present generation in India, we barely see families with more than one or two children and the act is very much spontaneous.

Along with his contemporaries; Samar Sen, Subhash Mukhopadhyay, Manindra Roy, Mangalacharan Chattopadhyay, Kiran Sankar Sengupta, Poet Nirendranath Chakraborty became a prominent entity amongst the new generation of Bengali poets and its readers. Later, for many years, Nirendranath Chakraborty efficiently edited one of the most prominent magazines for the children, 'Anandamela' (Joy-Carnival) before moving into the editorial board of the Anandabazar Patrika (leading news daily) as an advisor.

Sharp poetries such as, 'Ulanga Raja' (Naked King), 'Kolkatar Jishu (Jesus of Calcutta), Amalkanti (A Bengali name of a male) made Nirendranath Chakraborty famous and popular. His collection of poetries, 'Ulanga Raja' fetched him Saahitya Academy Award in 1974. In addition to several other prestigious awards, the poet was also conferred with honorary DLitt by the University of Calcutta.

Nirendranath Chakraborty has immensely guided the aspiring poets by authoring the book titled 'Kobitaar Class' (Poetry Class). Many scholars have written about meters and prosody of Bengali poetry; however, Nirendranath Chakraborty's teaching in this book remains as the simplest and the most eloquent. It is digestible with ease.

At the age of 93, Nirendranath Chakraborty still prevails as one of the living legends and an authority of Bengali literature. May he remain within us for many more years.

Fourth Child (Choturtho Santaan)
Nirendranath Chakraborty

Fourth Child

Two or three children at the most, that's it!
Sensing this slogan of dusking civilization,
The fourth child, inside the room
Facing the wall
You have been sitting in dejection.
In anger, perhaps in sadness, or may be in shame?
Your wide eyes at times fulminate,
Cloudy shadows sometimes, plummet.
The entire world conspiring against you, today,
Yet you yearn for the one,
Who would cherish you.

Who desires you?
Forbiddance along the path, shut doors all around.
Unwelcomed offshoot,
Crop of momentary reckless mistake
Fourth child, whom do you belong to?

Two or three children at the most, that's it!
Insult inflicted crease on your face, the fourth child of civilization,
In hysteric, abruptly you exit your room
Onto the thoroughfare
You rise in the open,
You slant gun aiming that derision.
Throng as well as clunkers standstill, establishments
Begin to yowl in fright.
Perchance they realize,
In the imminent war against all of them
You are the most merciless gladiator;
Maybe they have learnt,
The world that didn't welcome you,
Adept you are, you can disown it easily as well.

Choturtho Santaan

Duti kimbaa tinti baachchaa, byas!
Sabhyataar saayongkaaleen ei slogaaner artho bujhey niye,
Choturtho santaan, tumi gharer bhitorey
Deowaaler dikey mukh rekhey
Goom hoye bosey aachho.
Krodhey, naaki duhkkhey, naaki aboggae?
Aayata chokkhur modhye kakhono bidyut-jwaalaa kheley jaay,
Kakhono megher chhaayaa nemey aasey.
Tomaar biruddhey aaj jotbaddho samasto songsaar,
Tobuo cheyechho tumi taakey,
Je tomaakey chaay.

Ke tomaakey chaay?
Pathey-pathey nishedhaagyaa, dikey dikey niruddha duyaar.
Abaanchhito phol,
Asatarko muhurter bhraantir phasol
Choturtho santaan, tumi kaar?

Duti kimbaa tinti baachchaa, byas!
Apomaaney bikrito mukher rekhaa, sabhyataar choturtho santaan,
Hathhaat kakhon tumi ghar thekey unmaader moto
Raajpathey
Beriye esechho,
Bonduk tulechho oi bidruper dikey.
Janataa o jaanbaahon themey jaay, protisthhaanguli
Aatongkey chitkaar korey othhey.
Hoyto bujhechhey taaraa,
Aasanna diner juddhey tumi-i taader
Sob thekey khamaaheen pratidwandee;
Hoyto jenechhey,
Je-prithibee tomaakey chaayni,
Tumio akleshey taakey ghaarey dhorey jaahaannaamey thheley ditey paaro.

Sukanta Bhattacharya (1926 – 1947)

Sukanta Bhattacharya came to be known as a poet only after his death. Perhaps, one of the shortest-lived poets, Sukanta Bhattacharya was born in Kolkata on August 15, 1926. His parents migrated from Kotalipara in Faridpur (near Dhaka) – now Bangladesh. Sukanta Bhattacharya's father owned a publishing house named 'Saaraswat Library.' Later it turned out to be one of the prominent publishing houses in Kolkata. Sukanta Bhattacharya was the second child out of the seven sons, however, he was the first born to his mother Suniti Bhattacharya. Sukanta's father, Nibaran Chandra Bhattacharya and his first wife Saraju Bhattacharya had one son, Manomohan Bhattacharya. Sukanta shared a very cordial relationship with his stepmother and stepbrother.

Sukanata Bhattacharya's inclination towards writing manifested at a very early age. His first short story was published in school magazine, 'Parichoy' (Introduction). He attended Kamala Vidyamandir, a local primary school in Bagbazar (actual pronunciation is Bugbaazaar). Later, another of his writings, on the life of Swami Vivekananda was published in a magazine called 'Shikha' (Flame), edited by none other than Bijon Bhattacharya. Bijon Bhattacharya was one of the most prominent playwrights, dramatists and actors of the time. Sukanta Bhattacharya moved onto Beleghata Deshbandhu High School, following completion of primary education, however, wasn't successful in completing matriculation (High School).

At the age of 18, in 1944, Sukanta Bhattacharya joined the Communist Party of India. The party launched a daily newspaper, 'Swaadhinataa' (Independence) in 1946 and appointed Sukanta Bhattacharya as the editor of its youth section, 'Kishore Sabhaa.' However, Sukanta didn't live long enough to serve as the editor for too long. Suffering from tuberculosis, he died in a hospital on May 13, 1947, at the age of 20.

A staunch freedom loving person, Sukanta Bhattacharya, didn't live to witness India's independence declaration on August 15th of the same year. If lived, he would have been exactly 21 years of age on the day, India attained its independence.

Poet Subhash Mukhopadhyay, was a close friend of Sukanta Bhattacharya. Following Sukanta Bhattacharya's demise, Subhash Mukhopadhyay helped the family in publishing a collection of Sukanta's poetries. It was published by Saaraswat Library, his father's publishing house. Going through numerous editions, the complete collection of Sukanta Bhattacharya's poetries in one volume remains alive even today.

It is incredible, a boy, at such young age, felt the pain of his motherland and its people so deeply. And he expressed the feelings profoundly through his writings. A few lines from his poetry Chhaarpatra (Passport or Permit to Move) states, "Arrival of the newborn calls for his space. We must vacate this dilapidated world carrying death and debris over our shoulders. Will depart – yet as long as I am alive, I will set forth efforts towards removing all rubbish from this world. I will make this earth livable for the children. It is my promise to the newborn." A promise we all ought to take yet fail at miserably. This poetry became iconic in Bengali poetry. Another poetry 'Hey Mahaajiban" (O Great Life) states, "Poetry, I set you free today. The world struck with hunger is only prosaic. The poetic full moon appears to be a burnt bread."

"Matchstick or Deshlaai Kaathhi" is one such poetry as well. Sukanta Bhattacharya speaks in this poetry being a match stick. Allegorically, he associates each match stick with a destitute, impoverished human who possesses tremendous strength and power within. He talks about all the match sticks to gather and collectively become the volcanic power where they would not go unnoticed or ignored ever again.

Another legendary soul of Bengal, Sukanta's contemporary, lyricist and composer Salil Chowdhury (1923 – 1995) composed several poetries of Sukanta Bhattacharya into songs. These songs sung by Hemanta Mukhopadhyay (1920 – 1989) are evergreen. So is poet Sukanta Bhattacharya. A life of only 20 short years influenced the second half of the 20th century Bengal in a profound way.

Matchstick (Deshlaai Kaathi)
Sukanta Bhattacharya

Matchstick

I am an itsy-bitsy matchstick
Quite negligible, perchance I remain unseen:
Yet let it be known
Explosive is stirring upon my face –
Heart is swelling to be inflamed;
I am a matchstick.

Remember the hubbub on that day?
Corner of the room engulfed in flame –
Aftermath of irreverently tossing me un-doused!
I burnt down countless dwellings,
Bountiful palaces into ashes
Me alone – a tiny-little matchstick.

Likewise, jillions of towns, countless states we can ruin
Yet will you continue to snub us?
Forgot? Even recently –
En masse we sparked inside one single box;
You jolted –
We heard piteous cry out of your paled faces.

We are infinite power
You sensed it umpteen times;
Then why fail to fathom,
Captive in your pockets, we will not remain
We will free ourselves, we will disperse
To cities, suburbs, hamlets – horizon to horizon.

Repeatedly we're alight, in utter contempt –
You know it well enough!
Nonetheless, you are clueless:
On when we will ignite –
All of us – once and for all!

Deshlaai Kaathhi

Aami ektaa chhotto deshlaaier kaathhi
Eto naganya, hoyto chokheo pori naa:
Tobu jeno
Mukhey aamaar uskhush korchhey baarud –
Bukey aamaar jwoley uthhbaar duranto uchchhwaas;
Aami ektaa deshlaaier kaathhi.

Mone aachhey sedin hulusthool bedhechhilo?
Gharer koney jwoley uthhechhilo aagun –
Aamaakey abogyaabharey naa-nibhiye chhurey phelaay!
Kato ghorkey diyechhi puriye,
Kato praasaadke korechhi dhulisaat
Aami ekaai – chhotto ektaa deshlaai kaathhi.

Emoni bohu nagor, bohu raajyokey ditey paari chhaarkhaar korey
Tobuo abogyaa korbey aamaader?
Mone nei? Ei sedin –
Aamraa sabaai jwoley uthhechhilaam eki baaksey;
Chomkey uthhechhiley –
Aamraa shunechhilaam tomaader bibarno mukher aartonaad.

Aamaader kee aseem shokti
Taa to anubhab korechho baarongbaar;
Tobu keno bojho naa,
Aamraa bondee thaakbo naa tomaader pocketey pocketey,
Aamraa beriye porbo, aamraa chhoriye porbo
Shohorey, gonjey, graamey – diganto theke digantey.

Aamraa baarbaar jwoli, nitaanto abohelaay –
Taa to tomraa jaanoi!
Kintu tomraa to jaano naa:
Kabey aamraa jwoley uthhbo –
Sabaai – sheshbaarer moto!

Shamsur Rahman (1929 – 2006)

Shamsur Rahman, a columnist, a journalist and a poet, was born in 1929 in Pahartoli village in Narshingdi district of East Bengal (now Bangladesh). He was the fourth child out of thirteen. Following his matriculation (High School graduation), he entered college, however, dropped out from his Bachelor's studies. Three years later he completed Bachelor's degree and subsequently completed Master's degree in English literature from Dhaka University. A studious pupil, Shamsur Rahman ranked 2nd in his Master's degree.

Shamsur Rahman was deeply influenced by Rabindranath Tagore and Kazi Nazrul Islam. At the age of eighteen, Shamsur Rahman began to write poetry and other articles. Around 1949, his poetry 'Unishsho Unopanchaas' (Nineteen forty-nine) was published in 'Sonar Bangla' (Golden Bengal) magazine edited by eminent personality Nalinikishore Guho. Perhaps this was his first published poetry. Shamsur Rahman's first collection of poetry, 'Prathom Gaan Dwitiyo Mrittyur Aagey' (First Song Prior to the Second Death) was published in 1960. Shamsur Rahman's verses are primarily free in nature and often reflect resemblance with Jibanananda Dash's style.

Shamsur Rahman depicted relationship issues, humanism, and rebellious outcries in his poetries. However, as the region (East Bengal) went through political crisis during the 1960s, he didn't fail to pen its stories. Muktijuddha (Freedom Fight) of Bangladesh (late 60s – early 70s) turned into a subject matter for many of his writings as well.

Shamsur Rahman had a long career as a journalist. He launched his work life in 1957 as a co-editor of English Daily, 'Morning News' published from Dhaka. He also worked as the joint editor of Weekly 'Bichitra' (Variety) since 1973. Eventually he became the editor of 'Dainik Bangla' (Bangla Daily) in 1977. He was highly vocal against Bangladesh President Ershad's governance of the country. As a direct result of this opposition, under the influence of the president and the owners of Dainik Bangla, a new position of 'Chief Editor' was created overnight. Thus, his executive authority as the editor of the newspaper was taken away. In 1987, he protested this interference in free press by the government and resigned. He worked as the editor of a monthly literary magazine, 'Adhunaa' (Now-a-days) for a couple of years and also edited Weekly 'Muldhaaraa' (Mainstream) in 1989.

Otherwise a quiet and reserved personality, Shamsur Rahman, turned out to be highly outspoken against the religious fundamentalism in Bangladesh during the 1990s. Religious fundamentalism and reactionary nationalism has been active in Bangladesh for long. It has not only threatened the progressive outlooks, but also engaged in several killings of progressive minded personalities. Voices against religious fundamentalism become the enemies of the fundamentalists. Numerous people have been murdered by the fundamentalists. Murder attempts have been made on many others by the same factions. Shamsur Rahman wasn't spared either. In January of 1999, poet Shamsur Rahman was brutally attacked by the members of Harkat Ul Jihad Al Islami group. With help from the neighbors, his life was saved, however, his wife sustained severe injury. Neighbors nabbed the attackers and handed them over to the authorities.

In his poetry, "A Human Being or Ekjon Lok", Shamsur Rahman writes about a life of an apparent ordinary man. This man is the topic of discussion by all. Though he is benign to all, yet no one can spare him from their negative criticism. Leading an unconventional life, poetic by nature, this man is absorbed in immateriality. Perhaps that makes him a target of all. Nonetheless, the man is free of fear and warmly welcoming. Satirical in tone, this poetry perhaps takes a successful shot at the hypocrisy of our so-called society and its norms.

Shamsur Rahman received numerous awards and recognitions, including Bangla Academy Award in 1969 and Ananda Puraskar (conferred annually by the Anandabazar group of publications) in 1994. Author of over sixty books, Shamsur Rahman passed away from heart and kidney ailments in 2006 in Dhaka, Bangladesh.

Interested readers may find an in-depth knowledge of Shamsur Rahman's life and his writings in 'Shamsur Rahman: Nihsango Sherpa' (Shamsur Rahman: The Lonely Climber) written by eminent author, Humayun Azad.

A Human Being (Ekjon Lok)
Shamsur Rahman

A Human Being

He is no one – not a celebrity.
Yet he is discussed non-stop
By the puzzled folks of locality.

Nowhere the man has his dwelling.
Oomph of life wanders in dust,
Vain spindle his hands keep spinning.

Standoffish life he vanguards.
Mill-owner to village-superior –
No one is able to slumber;
As if there's a chip on his shoulder.

Public says, as well as me
He munches crunchy sunshine,
Moonlight being his favorite sip.
He lights up chiliads of lamps
Puts them out based on his whim.

He roams in garments of cloud
In neighborhood he strolls around.
Stone-caves don't make him winded
Answers door, if hasps are tapped.

Yet people complain and impugn:
The man wastes whole day in sleep,
Snugging pillow made out of moon.

Ekjon Lok

Loktaar nei kono naamdaak.
Tobu taar katha astoprahor
Bhebe lokjan abaak bebaak.

Loktaar nei konokhaaney thhaai.
Jibon lagno pather dhulaay,
Haatey ghorey taar aleek laataai.

Lokta karur sate-paache nei.
Gaayer morol, miler maalik –
Tobu ghum nei karur chokhei;
Loktaar kaadhey achin shalik.

Baley dashjoney ebong aamiyo
Roddur khaay lokta chibiye,
Jyotsnao taar saadher paaniya.
Hajar Pradip jwaalaay aabaar
Moner kheyaale dyay ta nibiye.

Megher kaamij shorirey chaapiye
Haatey, ese basey bhadroparay.
Pathurey guhaay parena hapiye
Se-o sara dyay korar naaraay.

Tobu dashjoney jaanaay naalish:
Lokta ghumaay saradinamaan,
Kachhey tene niye chaader baalish.

Ants (Piprey)
Shankha Ghosh

Ants

Ahem! Ants, may your wings begin to spread
No more can I endure thee!
Trailing   Trailing   Trailing heads
No more can I sustain to see.

Pantry full of food are there, they are for me to devour,
Why do you gobble? Detestable wickedly evil!
Pantry, plate, balcony, book, even table covered,
Peaceful bed, dead of night, that too you will?

Um! Ants, where is your home? Hover
Over there, else,
Plunge in Jamuna (river),
Or swing around the engulfing flames –
Unfurl the wings   Let wings unfurl   May your wings spread
Ugh! Ants, no more am I able to tolerate.

Piprey

Piprey re, tor pakha uthhuk
Aami je aar soitey paari naa!
Saaribondee   saaribondee   saaribondee mukh
Aami je aar dekhtey paari naa.

Almaaritey khaabaar aachhey, kintu se to aamaar janya raakhaa,
Tui keno taa khaas? Bishree badobhyaas!
Aalmaari, plate, baaraandaa, boi, ujaar tebildhhaakaa,
Gobheer raater bichhaanaataao chaas?

Piprey re, tor baasaa kothaay? Uriye diye paakhaa
Seikhaaney ja, noy,
Jhaap de jamunaay,
Noiley mosto aagun jwele coturdhaarey naach
Paakhaa uthhuk   paakhaa uthhuk   paakhaa uthhuk tor
Piprey re, aar soitey paari naa.

Shankha Ghosh (1932 –)

Shankha Ghosh, a poet of extraordinary caliber, was born in 1932 in Chandpur district (previously part of greater Comilla district and now part of Chittagong division), in East Bengal, now Bangladesh. He is considered to be one of the most prolific writers of Bengal and a living authority on Tagore literature.

Shankha Ghosh obtained his bachelor's degree in Bengali literature and language from Presidency College in 1951 and completed Master's degree in the same from University of Calcutta in 1954. An educator by profession, Shankha Ghosh taught at various colleges throughout his career. Later he joined the renowned Jadavpur University as a faculty of Bengali literature and retired from there in 1992. He is one of the few Bengali authors who participated in International Writing Program's Fall Residency at the University of Iowa, USA in 1967.

So far, Shankha Ghosh has authored over 60 books, however, not all of them are collection of poetry. A versatile author Shankha Ghosh writes in nearly all forms of literature including story, essay, rhyme, translation and much more. His profound understanding of literature and poetic meters are reflected in all of his creations. Externally a soft-spoken individual Shankha Ghosh uses his pen as a sword when needed. In recent times, his eloquent yet pun intended rhymes and poetries found its way in people's heart as he brought some of the whimsical decisions of the current ruling party in West Bengal, into focus. Though politically unaffiliated, Shankha Ghosh always found his polite ways to profess against social evils and injustices. His poetry encompasses humanity first, however, often reflects deeper philosophical perspective in a scholarly manner.

His poetry "Ants or Piprey" in this collection, reflects one such conscience. This poetry can be interpreted in many ways and different readers may connect with different emotions in it. I see a sublime pathos in this poetry. On surface it talks on behalf of a helpless person, who is wishing (cursing) all the intolerable ants to grow their wings, just so that they can be drawn to the fire and subsequently burn to death. The person is exasperated by the ants as they continue to forcibly and relentlessly occupy the entire living space, sparing no room for the individual. The individual cannot battle to eradicate or exterminate all the ants. Therefore, helplessly only prays for the ants to die in fire. Allegorically it can reflect many analyses. It can be viewed under a political microscope as well.

A simplified version of Bengali poetics and meters, 'Chhander Baaraandaa' (Balcony of meters), authored by Shankha Ghosh is a priceless possession for the entire Bengali speaking community. The book elaborately discusses meters used in Bengali verses from the time of Michael Madhusudan Dutta to poet Bishnu Dey. His eloquent explanations help readers to comprehend the aesthetics of meters in poetry in an easier way.

For his tremendous contribution in literature, Shankha Ghosh has received numerous awards and recognition including Saahitya Academy Award (Academy of literature) in 1977, Rabindra Puraskar (Rabindra Award) in 1989. In 1999, he received a second Saahitya Academy Award for translation of noted playwright Girish Karnad's 'Taledanda' (original in Kannada language) into Bengali 'Rakta-Kalyaan' (Death by Beheading). Shankha Ghosh was conferred by various recognitions as well, including 'Desikottam' title by Visva-Bharati University in 1999, honorary DLitt by Vidyasagar University in 2010, honorary DLitt from Indian Institute of Engineering Science and Technology, Shibpur in 2015, Padmabhusan by the Indian government in 2011 and Gyanpeethh (Receptacle of Knowledge) Award in 2016.

Wish the copious poet many more years of creative life to continue to enrich our treasure.

Shakti Chattopadhyay (1933 – 1995)

One of the most imitated and adored poets of Bengal, Shakti Chattopadhyay was born in 1933 in a village in south 24 Parganas district of West Bengal called Baharu. His literary abilities became evident at an early age, though he still struggled to make ends meet. At sixteen, he launched a hand written literary magazine titled, 'Pragati' (Progress). Pragati soon turned into a print magazine with its name changed to 'Bahnisikha' (Tongue of Fire or Flame). His maternal uncle, who was also his guardian, promised him a job as an accountant on completion of his bachelor's degree. Hence, following matriculation (High School Graduation), in 1951, Shakti Chattopadhyay Joined the City College to major in commerce. But half way, though, left City College to major in Bengali literature and language at Presidency College. Eventually, though he quit Presidency College too and never received his Bachelor's degree.

Due to his unruly behavior, he was forced to leave his maternal uncle's home. In 1956, at the age of 23 he moved to a slum in Ultadanga in north Calcutta. The same year his poetry, 'Yama' (Yama – the Hindu God of Death) was published in Buddhadeb Bosu's magazine. Buddhadeb Bosu invited him to attend Jadavpur University in its newly formed Comparative Literature course. Shakti Chattopadhyay joined, but once again, left the university without completing the course.

The poet needed money badly for his survival. He began to work as a store assistant at Saxby Pharma Limited, as well as, as a tutor at Bhowanipur Tutorial Home, a popular student-coaching center. Subsequently he started a business that did not last long and he joined Hind Motors automobile manufacturing company as a junior executive. He truly indulged in a wayward lifestyle and couldn't last in any job for long.

His association with the Communist Party of India met with similar fate. As a freshman in City College, he joined the party in 1951 only to sever all ties with it in 1958. Later he criticized the communist party as well as the leftist ideology in some of his poetries.

During the early 60s he met Allen Ginsberg, a materialistically disillusioned hippie from the United States who had come to India in search of Indian sojourn. Peter Orlovsky, Gary Snyder and Joanne Kyger joined this radical poet. They all smoked marijuana and roamed the streets of Kolkata, especially the crematoriums where Allen wished to witness the transformation process from dead flesh and bone to ashes. Shakti Chattopadhyay became one of them. In 1961, he began a new literary movement with three other likeminded poets, Malay Roy Choudhury, Samir Roychoudhury and Debi Roy. It was known as the 'Hungry Generation Movement.' Eventually he denounced Hungry Movement and left its association. Many criticized Hungry Generation Movement as being uncivil, pornographic and obscene.

In 1962, Shakti Chattopadhyay's first collection of poetry 'Hey Prem Hey Noihshabdo' (O Love O Silence) was published. He wrote the poetries of this collection while staying with Samir Roychoudhury in Chaibasa, now in the state of Jharkhand. There he fell in love with Samir's sister-in-law Minakshi. Later they married which resulted in a relatively settled life for Chattopadhyay.

Through all his ups and downs, Shakti Chattopadhyay remained a prolific writer. Tirelessly he wrote poetries culminating into nearly two thousand verses. Additionally, he wrote novels, features, and columns. For several years he worked at Anandabazar Group of Publications. Following his retirement from Anandabazar, he joined the renowned Visva-Bharati University as a faculty. He passed away in Shantiniketan (the village where Tagore's Viva-Bharati is situated) in 1995.

In "O Ever Venerable Pyre or O Chiropranamyo Agni" he recites to the same fire, that he paid a visit to with the other bohemian poet Allen Ginsberg. He invokes in this hymn like poetry the ultimate surrender and submission of human end. Graciously he petitions the fire to accept him segment by segment as he describes each limb and his resolution with them. This poetry is one of his most famous verses.

Shakti Chattopadhyay received numerous awards and recognitions including Ananda Puraskaar (Ananda Award) and Saahitya Academy Award (Academy of Literature).

O Ever Venerable Pyre (O Chiropranamyo Agni)
Shakti Chattopadhyay

O Ever Venerable Pyre

O ever venerable pyre

Blaze me.

Begin with the two legs that are inert,

Then the hands that are devoid of devotion and goodness.

Now the noosing arms fondled by chill flowers,

Now the duty desolated shoulder,

Once done with them – debouch to existence,

Pause a moment, eradicate next

The truth-lie-hue-blanched quiet receptacle of wisdom.

Safeguard the two eyes please

Perhaps they are

Yet to see some more.

Once wailing emptied, destroy those oculi,

Don't burn the floral garland, fragrant tousled bouquet,

Caressing touch, withal affixed to it still.

Let it float in the Ganges unchallenged, wayward…

O ever venerable pyre

Blaze me.

O Chiropranamyo Agni

O chiropranamyo agni

Aamaakey poraao.

Prathomey poraao oi paa duti jaa chalachchhaktiheen,

Taarpor je-haatey aaj prem porichchhannotaa kichhu nei.

Ekhon baahur faadey phooler barof,

Ekhon kaadher parey dayitwaheenotaa,

Oder puriye eso jeebaner kaachhey,

Daaraao lahomaa, taarpor dhwangso karo

Satyamithyaa rangey-shwetey stabdho gyanpeethh.

Rakkhaa karo duti chokh

Hoyto taader

Ekhono dekhaar kichhu kichhu baaki aachhey.

Ashrupaat shesh holey nasto koro aakhi,

Puriyonaa phoolmaalaa stabak sugandhey aaluthaalu,

Priyo karsparsho or gaaye legey aachhey.

Gangaajaley bhesey jetey diyo okey mukto, swechchhaachaaree…

O chiropranamyo agni

Aamaakey poraao.

Conversation 11 (Kathopokathan 11)
Purnendu Patri

Conversation 11

Purnendu Patri authored 'Kathopokathan' as a collection of poetries with 41 poems. Each poem is separated by serial numbers from 1 through 41. All the poems in this book are written in conversational form. The entire series imply intimacy between two confidants named Shubhankar[1] and Nandini[2]. This poem is expected to be read like reading dialogues in a play.

~ Lately you have been smoking too much Shubhankar.
~ Tossing it right away.
  But in return?
~ Extremely greedy. As if you never had eaten?
~ Ate.
  But those were minim for my hunger.
  I can chaw the entire Kolkata[3] in one bite.
  Slitting the sky into pieces like an omelet
  Tearing all the stars small and paltry like peanuts
  Crumbling the mountains like crunchy papad[4]
  And the Ganges?[5]
  That's just a glass of sherbet.[6]
~ I suppose. Very manly.
~ It's true.
  I am this fierce explosion for the world.
  However, I am just a milk drinking infant when next to you
  When I am with you, I turn into a mutilated beggar of footpath
  One paisa[7], half a paisa or a loaf of bread at the most
  Nothing more can I yank away.
~ Liar.
~ How is so?
~ Did you not disrobe me fully by yanking away my saree[8] the other day?
~ I might have.
  Can a beggar not wish to be a robber for a day?

---

[1] Shubhankar is a random popular Bengali male name. Loosely translated in English, Shubhankar means beneficial or favorable or auspicious.
[2] Nandini is a common female name. Loosely translated in English, Nandini means a daughter or delighting or pleasing or charming.
[3] Kolkata is one of the most prominent cosmopolitan cities in India, situated in West Bengal.
[4] Papad is a popular Indian snack. It is rolled into a round shaped thin layer of dough primarily from grinded pigeon-peas. It is more commonly known as Papadum.
[5] Ganges or Ganga is the most prominent (romanticized as well) river in India stretching from the Himalayas to the Bay of Bengal.
[6] Sherbet is a cold drink of sweetened and diluted fruit juice.
[7] Paisa is a monetary subunit (coin) of the rupee or taka, primarily in India, Bangladesh, Pakistan and Nepal.
[8] Saree is a garment of southern Asian women that consists of several yards of lightweight cloth draped so that one end forms a skirt and the other a head or shoulder covering.

Kathopokathan 11

~ *Tumi aajkaal baro cigarette khaachchho Shubhankar.*
~ *Ekhuni chhurey pheley dichchhi.*
  Kintu taar badoley?
~ *Baddo hyanglaa. Jeno khaaoni kakhono?*
~ *Kheyechhi.*
  Kintu aamaar khider kaachhey sesob nosyi.
  Ei Kolkatake ek khaablaay chibiye khetey paari aami.
  Aakaashtaakey omeleter moto chirey chirey
  Nakshotrogulokey chineybaadaamer moto tuktak korey
  Paahaargulokey papar bhaajaar moto marmoriye
  Aar Ganga?
  Se to ek glass sarbat.
~ *Thaak. Khub beerpurush.*
~ *Satyi taai.*
  Prithibeer kaachhey aami ei rakomi bhoyonkar bisphoran.
  Kebol tomaar kaachhey elei dudher baalak
  Kebol tomaar kaachhey elei footpather nulo bhikhaaree
  Ek poysaa, aadh poysaa kimbaa ek tukro paaurutir beshee
  Aar kichhu chhiniye nitey paari naa.
~ *Mithyuk.*
~ *Keno?*
~ *Sedin aamaar sarbaanger shaari dhorey taan maaroni?*
~ *Hotey paarey.*
  Bhikhareeder ki daakaat hotey ichchhey korbey naa ekdino?

Purnendu Patri (1933 – 1997)

A versatile creative personality, Purnendu Patri was born in 1933 in Howrah, West Bengal, India. He was inclined to artistic activities since a very early age. In some of his books, he spelled his name as Purnendu Pattrea.

Following his schooling, Purnendu Patri joined the Indian Art College in Kolkata to pursue a degree in art. However, he manifested as a prolific poet much earlier. His first collection of poetries 'Ek Muthho Rode' (A Handful Sunshine) was published in 1951 when he was only eighteen years old. In addition to poetry, Purnendu Patri also wrote rhymes, novels, travelogues, essays, researched features, stories and screenplays. He was a noted critic as well. His first novel 'Daarer Moynaa' (Perched Mynah) was published in 1958. This novel fetched him 'Manik Puraskaar' (Maanik Award).

Romantic in all aspects, Purnendu Patri's amorous writings poetically influenced many, especially the youth of the time. Through his subtle strokes of expression, he allowed fanciful imagination to roam freely and endlessly. His poetries were recited by the elocutionists allover. Even his bohemian appearance became iconic. Purnendu Patri was the symbol of romanticism in his time.

Purnendu Patri immersed himself in creativity in many mediums. For a long period of time, he reigned as the most prominent illustrator and designer of books. No leading author of his time missed the opportunity to obtain cover design, rendered by Purnendu Patri. Even today, Purnendu Patri remains alive through those amaranthine cover designs. In addition to cover designs, he illustrated many books including his own poetry books. Wizardry of his artistic caliber has been proclaimed through his works. It appears as if he was always competing with himself as he ceaselessly created higher quality of work than before, though he never detoured from his iconic style.

Purnendu Patri was fascinated by the era of Rajas (kings/Royals) in and around Kolkata as well as of Bengal. He did extensive research on old Calcutta and its way of life. This research was eloquently served to his readers in a collection of essays. Perhaps his artistic gifts made him a master in portraying visuals through his writings.

During late 1960s, Purnendu Patri became interested in filmmaking. Between 1967 and 1982, he directed eleven feature films. His film rendition of Rabindranath Tagore's 'Streer Patro' (Wife's Letter) won him national award for best feature film in Bengali in 1972. He wrote the screenplay for this film as well.

Purnendu Patri wrote several collections under the title of 'Kathopokathan' (Conversation). "Conversation 11 or Kathopokathan 11" is part of the first collection. In this first collection, published by Ananda Publishers in 1981, Purnendu Patri wrote in the introduction, "Once, in this city of Kolkata, 45 years old Shubhankar fell in love with a lightening woman named Nandini. I accompanied them daily in their guerilla warfare like saga of love. And every day, I jotted down their Abir coated conversation in my notebook (Abir is a colored perfumed powder applied during the annual Hindu festival of Holi). Shubhankar is now 50 years old. And Nandini perhaps is now caged on a golden divan of extreme terrible happiness. The river as well as the ferryboat between the two are now lost. Once, I contemplated floating away these pieces of paper in the dark storm. But then I felt, the ones who love, the ones who encolour the horizon with a different glow of twilight through the smoldering love affairs of theirs, perhaps would reflect their own obscure love stories in these notes. I even visualized those faces that years after my demise would cultivate this monsoon of love in their blood stream. Hence, I wasn't able to callously put to death these pieces of papers."

The evergreen poet passed away in 1997 in Kolkata.

Just For Poetry (Shudhu Kobitaar Janya)
Sunil Gangopadhyay

Just For Poetry

Just for verses this nascence of mine,
This recreation is just for rhyme
Just for odes my solitary chilled dusk
Just for quatrain, my journey – the globe across
Glimpse of unwinking reposed glance;
Just for sestina – woman you enhance
Just for poetry all these bloodshed,
Over the cloud Gangetic cascade
Just for rune I covet – life to perpetuate
Though life of human fully disquiet,
Just for you – Oh poesy
I brushed off my immortality.

Shudhu Kobitaar Janya

Shudhu kobitaar janya ei janmo, shudhu kobitaar
Janya kichhu khelaa, shudhu kobitaar janya ekaa him sandhyebelaa
Bhuban periye aasaa, shudhu kobitaar janya
Apalok mukhoshreer shaanti ek jhalok;
Shudhu kobitaar janya tumi naari, shudhu
Kobitaar janya eto raktopaat, meghe gaangyeo propaat
Shudhu kobitaar janya aaro dirghodin beNche thaakte lobh hoy
Maanusher moto khovmoy beNche thaakaa, shudhu kobitaar
Janya aami amaratya taachchhilya korechhi.

Sunil Gangopadhyay (1934 – 2012)

Sunil Gangopadhyay, by no means can be labeled as just a poet. He wrote more proses than poetries. A truly colorful personality, Sunil Gangopadhyay was born in Faridpur of present day Bangladesh in 1934 but his family moved to Kolkata (Calcutta) when he was very young. Following India's independence and partition, his ancestral home became part of Bangladesh and the travel between the two countries became restricted per international protocols. This partition caused him much anguish, which he poured in many of his writings.

Following his schooling, Sunil Gangopadhyay studied in various colleges eventually earning his Master's degree in Economics from University of Calcutta in 1954. However, while still in college, in 1953 he launched the iconic literary magazine 'Krittibaas' (Krittibas was the author of Ramayana, the Hindu epic. Krittibas is also a name of lord Shiva, one of the Hindu trinity). With time, this magazine became synonymous with many poet's poetical baptism, transforming them from an amateur to a seasoned entity. Though the magazine occasionally went into hibernation, however, it managed to reemerge following brief pauses. Following Sunil Gangopadhyay's demise, Krittibas reappeared and is currently being published under the supervision of his wife Swati Gangopadhyay.

Like his close friend, poet Shakti Chattopadhyay, Sunil Gangopadhyay also led a bohemian life and met with poet Allen Ginsberg while Ginsberg visited Kolkata. Ginsberg later mentioned Sunil Gangopadhyay in his 'September on Jessore Road' poetry. Similarly, Sunil Gangopadhyay mentioned Ginsberg in a few of his writings. Later Kabir Suman (Suman Chattopadhyay – noted Bengali ballad lyricist-composer-singer) mentioned Sunil Gangopadhyay in his popular song 'Gariahatar mor' (The corner at Gariahat). Sunil Gangopadhyay soon became synonymous with the existence of Kolkata. The poet served as the honorary sheriff of Calcutta for a few years too.

Sunil Gangopadhyay authored a greater volume of literature when compared to most other Bengali authors. He has over 200 published books and the Library of Congress holds over 100 of these titles. Sunil Gangopadhyay wrote under several pen-names, especially Neellohit, Sanatan Pathhak and Neel Upadhyay. Several of his short stories and novels were adopted into feature films. His novels, 'Aranyer Din-Raatri' (Days and Nights in the Forest) and 'Pratidwandi' (The Adversary) were rendered into film version by noted film director Satyajit Ray.

A luxuriant author, Sunil Gangopadhyay received several awards and recognitions including, Ananda Puraskaar (Ananda Award) in 1972, Bankim Puraskar (Award named after noted author Bankim Chandra Chattopadhyay) in 1983, Saahitya Academy Award (Academy of literature award) in 1984, a second time Ananda Puraskaar in 1989, Annadasankar Puraskar (Award named after noted author Annadasankar Ray) in 2003, Saraswati Samman (Award named after the Hindu goddess of knowledge Saraswati) in 2004.

Different than his contemporaries, Sunil Gangopadhyay developed a distinct style of his own in his poetry, depicting stories of love and other emotions through his poetries, often in free verse. Gangopadhyay's fictitious character 'Neera' appeared in many of his poetries and became an icon of romance. Neera is a woman who embodies the persona of a passionate lover, a friend, a mother as well as of a muse. She is a complete woman according to the poet. They meet, yet the affair never culminates into anything specific. These meetings are stimulus for the poet where Neera attributes bountifully only for the poet to wait eternally for the next stimuli. In his juvenile writings, Sunil Gangopadhyay introduced another character, 'Kakababu' (Uncle) who became very popular among his readers. Some of the Kakababu novels have been filmed as well.

In his poetry, "Just For Poetry or Shudhu Kobitaar Janya", Sunil Gangopadhyay affectionately expresses his deep-rooted relationship with poetry. Unequivocally he states, his life as well as his death and everything in between are inseparably intertwined with poetry. Though Gangopadhyay became famous mostly for his novels and stories, yet he declared, poetry was his first love.

Beside Rabindranath Tagore, one of the most celebrated literary personalities, Sunil Gangopadhyay passed away in Kolkata in 2012.

Apurba Dutta (1951 – 2016)

Poet Apurba Dutta was born in 1951 in Ranaghat, Nadia district, West Bengal, India. His family residence was situated on the bank of the river, Churnee. Picturesque backdrop of the river fascinated him since his childhood. Later he reflected this emotion in several of his writings including in his poetries. Seventh child among the ten siblings, Apurba Dutta acknowledged his mother, Latika Dutta for her attribution towards his inclination in literature since early childhood.

Following his schooling from Palchowdhury Higher Secondary School of Ranaghat in 1966 (it is a rare accomplishment to complete schooling at the age of 15), Apurba Dutta earned his Bachelor's degree in Political Science from Krishnanagar Government College, Krishnanagar, Nadia in 1969. Subsequently he completed Master's degree from University of Calcutta in 1971. Later, he pursued a second Master's degree in English literature at University of Calcutta and completed it in 1979. Additionally, he received a diploma in Journalism. His scholarly knowledge of Bengali, English and Sanskrit languages was profound. People fondly called him a walking-talking dictionary.

While working at a nationalized bank in Kolkata, Apurba Dutta fell in love with his colleague, Kaberi Das, also a student of literature. Kaberi inspired Apurba towards his literary persuasion. It was only after tying the nuptial knot with Kaberi in 1975, Apurba Dutta took serious interest in creative works. His writings appeared in various magazines, however, he waited until early 1990s to publish his first book. His deep passion in writing guided him in 2001 to take early voluntary retirement from his day job giving him finally the opportunity to immerse full time in literary works.

A man, full of endless wit, Apurba Dutta gained popularity primarily due to his rhymes and juvenile literature. In addition, he wrote poetries, essays, novels and stories. His rhyme 'Bangla-Tangla' (Bengali-Tengali) made him a famous personality. Numerous prominent elocutionists have recited this rhyme. It has also been recorded by many. Apurba Dutta himself recorded many of his poetries and rhymes. In a society as its culture gradually leans towards embracing western styles and its language, Apurba Dutta's satire in Bangla-Tangla rhyme sharply reminds the indigenous people the value of Bengali language as well as its beauty and its necessity.

Adored for his sense of humor, Apurba Dutta, the poet and elocutionist, was invited worldwide to recite his work. He traveled to many countries including Bangladesh, USA, Norway, Sweden, Denmark, Germany, Switzerland, France, Italy, Russia, Australia as an invited poet and elocutionist. Everywhere he went, his admirers (including other authors) found a deep-rooted friendship in his association.

"If I Go Away or Jodi Choley Jaai" is part of his last collection of poetries titled, 'Prem O Mrittyur Kobitaa' (Poetry of Love and Death), published just a few days before his demise. In this poetry, the poet had expressed his views on exiting life. As much as he liked to be amongst people and his loved ones, he reflected the same in this poetry. It wasn't that he planned out all details about his exit, nonetheless, he knew, the day would come someday. He wished to bid bye to all before departing for good.

Ironically, on his way to participate in a literary meet, Apurba Dutta suffered a massive cerebral hemorrhage and never regained consciousness. After remaining in coma for a couple of days, the poet passed away on a beautiful autumn morning in 2016, without the opportunity to bid goodbye to anyone.

Apurba Dutta authored approximately 50 books, nearly 30 of which were of rhymes and juvenile writings. He received numerous awards and recognitions including 'Abhigyan Award' conferred by Paschim Banga Bangla Academy (West Bengal Bengali Academy) and an award conferred by Shishu Saahitya Parishad (Association of Children Literature).

If I Go Away (Jodi Choley Jaai)
Apurba Dutta

If I Go Away

If I go away…
Bracing the momentary bridge if I go away
     If I go away leisurely in a single piece of cloth!

Sowing sorrow in no one, hatching harm on nobody
Smilingly if I can go away
     Then I would.

If I go away…
Where, how, why, with whom
     Or when
It's not that, these thoughts don't cross my mind
Nevertheless, nothing has been decisively sorted yet
Have to go – for the nonce let this much be written.

Through ifs and buts suppose I really go away
Thenceforth I wish to bid bye to all;
Like Gautam Buddha – hush hush
     Tiptoed… solitary not…

Jodi Choley Jaai

Jodi choley jaai…
Muhoorter saako dhorey Jodi choley jaai
     Jodi choley jaai ghumchokhey ek bastrey!

Kaukey kasto naa diye, kaaror kono anisto naa korey
Haastey haastey Jodi choley jetey paari
     Tabey jaabo.

Jodi choley jaai…
Kothaay kee-bhaabey keno kaar songey
     Athobaa kakhan
Esob chintaa je mone aasey naa taa noy
Tabey kichhu sunishchit bhaabaa hoyni ekhon parjanta
Jetey habey – aapaatoto eituku likhey raakhaa jaak.

Jodi jodi korey jodi satyi-i choley jaai
Tabey jyano sabaaikey boley jetey paari;
Gautam Buddher moto chupi chupi
     Paaye paaye… ekaa ekaa noy…

New Precept (Notun Niyom)
Suvo Das Gupta

New Precept

Henceforth, cabinet passed the resolution:
Hereafter, cigarette pack akin, forehead of all humans
Shall have this inscribed – Staying alive is injurious to health.

Journalists afflicted ministers with arrowlike questions.
Old ministers, young ministers, active ministers, sleepy ministers
Together their answers gave an impression,
Which essentially meant –
If humans stay alive, will die from famine, die of disease, or in grief they will die,
In the hands of dacoits or in affray or in accidents they will die.
If stayed alive, humans will commit suicide – therefore,
Under the new precept, we wish to raise this awareness within humans,
That, staying alive is detrimental to health.
Eh mister; what has no beginning no end is termed a problem.
Problem is un-exterminable[1] – imperishable, unconquerable.
Therefore, in this new law, we also declare
The other name for life is problem.
Problem-free life, like no-salt omelet, is unpalatable.

Elephants and horses never brush teeth, yet their teeth always sparkle.
More so; elephant teeth are priceless like the speech of a non-political hero[2].
Humans brush teeth needlessly. Only bourgeois multi-national
Company strengthens from it. Dentist gains house and car
While human loses teeth at last.
All these indulgences, the new precept asks to discard.
Till now all research has shown – on the altar of god in all homes
Supreme venerable gods, through generations spanning over hundreds of years
Have been prevailing happily just with molasses, banana slice, cucumber, sugar candy
And turbid water of the river Ganges.
How can it harm humans if they adopt the same diet? Especially
Since we idolize and worship gods?
Therefore – in this new precept, our advice to embrace the 'divine-diet'[3]
Has been documented as well.

---

[1] The poet here used the word – Raktobeej. Raktobeej is a (Hindu) mythological demon. Like Lernaean Hydra (in Greek and Roman mythology), if anyone attempt to slay Raktobeej by cutting him and in that process if a drop of his blood falls on the ground, it would create a demon who is equally powerful as Raktobeej. Subsequently, if the newly created demon is attempted to be killed and if his blood drops on the ground, that would create numbers of new demons equally strong. Therefore, it is impossible to kill Raktobeej or his clan.

[2] Poet here used the expression, 'Maroder baat'. Marod means a man or a manly person. It is a colloquial expression in Bengali that means an irrevocable pledge by a manly person (which makes him a hero) is as priceless as an Elephant tusk or ivory.

[3] Majority of Hindus maintain an altar in their homes. Upon the altar they place images or idols of the gods they worship daily. Each day, they offer food and water to the worshipped gods and goddesses. The poet has referred to this ritual.

Notun Niyom

Atohpor montrisabhaay siddhaanto hoilo:
Ekhon thekey cigarette packeter moto sob maanusher kapaaleo
Likhey ditey habey – beche thaakaa swaasthyer pakkhhey haanikar.

Sangbaadikraa montrimashaaider prashnobaaney jarjorito korey tullen.
Probeen montri nobeen montri kormee montri ghumanto montri
Sakkoley galaa miliye jaa-sob jabaab dilen,
Taar saar kathaataa holo –
Beche thaakley maanush anaahaarey morbey, rogey morbey, shokey morbey,
Daakaater haatey baa daangaaye athobaa durghatonaaye morbey.
Beche thaakley maanush aatmohatyaao korbey – atoeb
Notun niyomey maanusher modhye ei sachetanotaar bikaash ghataatey chaai
Je, beche thaakaa swaasthyer pakkhey khaaraap.
Aarey mashaai jaar aadi anto nei taar naam samosyaa.
Samosyaa holo raktobeejer moto – amor aparaajeyo.
Taai notun aainey aamraa ekathaao ghoshonaa korechhi
Je jeebaner aar ek naam samosyaa.
Samosyaaheen jeeban nunbiheen omleter moto akhaadyo.

Haati ghoraay daat maajenaa, athocho taader dibyi jhakjhakey daat.
Haatir daat to non political 'maroder baat' er motoi mulyabaan.
Maanush khaamokaa daat maajey. Otey bourgeois multinational
Kompaanider shreebriddhi hoy. Dentistder baari gaari hoy
Maanush shesh parjantya foklaai hoye parey.
Notun niyomey ei sob baahulyo barjaner janya balaa hoyechhey.
A jaabat sameekkhaaye dekhaa gechhe – gharey gharey thhaakurer aasoner
Mahaamaanyo thhaakurraa baataasaa, chaapaakalaar tukro, sashaa, nokuldaanaa
Ebong gangaar gholaa jaley kaeksho bachhor purushaanukromey
Mahaasukhey din jaapon korchhen.
Maanush taader khaadyaabhyaas grahon korley khoti ki? Bishesato
Thhaakurgan jakhon aadorsho o pujyo?
Atoeb – aamaader notun niyomey 'debbhogyo' khaabaar paraamarsho-o aamraa
Lipibaddho korechhi.

Suvo Das Gupta (1951 –)

One of the most unconventional poets of Bengali poetry, Suvo Das Gupta was born in 1951 in Bhatpara of north 24 Parganas district, West Bengal, India. He grew up in lower-middle class joint family along with his cousins. As a child Suvo Das Gupta was involved in sports such as soccer and cricket. He is an adroit swimmer as well. However, he was attracted to movies, stage theater, songs and other artistic works from an early age.

After completing his schooling in 1969 from Amar Krishna Paathhshaalaa in Bhatpara, Suvo Das Gupta earned his Bachelor's degree from Goenka College of Commerce in 1972. Following this, he joined a nationalized Bank and worked there as a professional until his retirement in 2011. Though he associated himself with certain political ideologies, however, never joined any political party or activities directly.

His first poetry was published in his school magazine during his childhood. However, his matured writings didn't surface till much later. During the 1980s he developed acquaintance with legendary lyricist, composer and singer Salil Chowdhury (1923 – 1995) who inspired him greatly. It was only after this association, Suvo Das Gupta engaged himself seriously in writing. Eventually, in 1984, at the age of 33, his first collection of poetry was published as an audio album. Suvo Das Gupta gained instant popularity with this album and never looked back.

Suvo Das Gupta adopted a form of writing that didn't adhere with any known metrics or meters of conventional poetry. His focus was to free poetry from the cages of heavy words and difficult to understand formations. He wanted to make poetry readable and loveable by commoners who otherwise would not find poetry enjoyable. Since the very beginning, flagrantly he declared his creations as 'non-poetry' and this became virtually a trademark of Suvo Das Gupta's writings. However, by no means has Suvo Das Gupta ever expressed any enmity or derogation towards the traditional construction of poetry. As much as he finds relevance in his own style, he equally adores and admires the stringent poetics constructed by others. Nonetheless, sufferings of ordinary people, corruptions of ruling system, apathy and injustices in the society, find its simplest yet bold expressions through Suvo Das Gupta's poetry. His intense urge to stand by the needs of people makes him a peoples' person in every sense of the word.

Though Suvo Das Gupta gained enormous fame since 1984 with elocutionists continuing to record his poetry, however, his first collection of poetry in book form tilted 'Shudhu Tomaar Janya' (Just For You) was not published until 1996. An accomplished poet (of non-poetry), Suvo Das Gupta till date has authored 56 collections of poetry, 24 other published titles (other than poetry), 154 song albums (as lyricist) and 76 audio albums of poetry. There are virtually no prominent singers or elocutionists in Bengal who have not recorded Suvo Das Gupta's song or poetry. From popular modern singers like Manna Dey to eminent classical singers such as Pundit Ajay Chakrabarty and Ustad Rashid Khan, countless singers have immortalized Suvo Das Gupta's lyrics. He is one of the busiest lyricists of present day.

In his 'non-poetry', "New Precept or Notun Niyom" Suvo Das Gupta has brought forward the fallacy of governing general human life. He becomes fierce through extraordinary sarcasm about inept government as the government fails to secure basic means of survival for the general population. In a resourceful country like India, it is intolerable not to have adequate opportunity to meet the basic needs for a vast section of people. Suvo Das Gupta stands by the sufferers of economic inequality through his uncompromising penmanship. The unscrupulous characteristics of the ministers are surfaced in this non-poetry, as well as the manipulated helplessness of the common man.

For his sincere contributions to the life of the ordinary people through his writings, Suvo Das Gupta has been bestowed with numerous awards and recognitions. He received Gold Disk recognition in 1998 for one of his albums of non-poetry, Best Lyricist Awards in 2000, 2003, 2004 and in 2006. Recently in 2018, he received the Krittibaas Award.

Suvo Das Gupta is married to Ruma Das Gupta since 1979.

Why I Am Rayless (Keno Aami Andhokaar)
Joy Goswami

Why I Am Rayless

Why do I publish rayless gloom?
Over the cloud those carrion of star
Why do I roam still hauling on shoulder?
Snare to snare, why does my path
Entrap ofttimes? Pixie stranger's
Wings I rip, why do I wail aftermath
At home? Why do I? Why every night
To resurrect her life amiss mantra I recite?
Why by the bed does she braid her hair?
Why she cooks venom for me with utmost care?
As soon as zealously I turn her towards me
Again she is slain Oh dead she I see!
Gods, saints, ascetics in all domiciles
Everyone I know on footpath, leas, and aisles
Please tell me, you tell me, help me forthright
Despite this why tell me – why still I sight

A golden ladder upraised all the way to moon!

Joy Goswami's poetries perhaps, are the most emending creations of contemporary Bengali poetry. The contextual verve as well as merrymaking within his verses, carry an authentic imprint of Bengali culture and its intrinsic psyche. Thus, making it perhaps the most difficult to translate. Nonetheless, through the emotions of Bengal, he weaves a complete connectivity with human sentiments universally. However, an understanding of Bengali life would allow readers to savor the essence and aroma of his originals. The transcreated poetry here, contains a very rustic Bengali rhythm (similar to goddess Laxmi's panchali). If it is read in that rhythm, the rhythm itself becomes the rhyme.

Keno Aami Andhokaar

Keno aami andhokaar bishaad chhaapaai?
Keno aami mehge mrito taaraar shorir
Ekhono bahon korey niye choli kaadhey?
Keno baa aamaar raastaa faad thekey faadey
Giye parey baarbaar? Achenaa porir
Daanaa chhirey keno aami haahaakaar kori
Gharey ese? Keno kori? Keno roj raatey
Bhul mantro diye taar jeeban pheraai?
Keno se shajyaar paashey bosey chul baadhey?
Keno se aamaar janya jatney bish raadhey?
Jei taakey nijer dikey jor korey ghoraai
Pher se nihato ogo dekhi se mritaai!
Gharey gharey bhagobaan saadhu o joginee
Maathhey pathey footpaathey jaakey jaakey chini
Tumi balo, tumi balo, balo tomraai
Erpareo keno aami keno dekhtey paai

Ekti sonar moi uthhey gechhe chaadey!

Joy Goswami (1954 –)

A laudable scion in the land of prolific poets such as Rabindranath Tagore and Jibanananda Dash, Joy Goswami was born in 1954 in Kolkata, India. Joy lost his father at the age of eight leaving his mother to lead the family through a prolonged phase of severe financial struggle. In the 1960s Bengal, it wasn't easy for a woman to raise a family single handedly. This had its impact on Joy Goswami. In his eleventh grade he decided to quit school never to return to formal education again, though he later received two honorary D.Litt. conferred by University of Calcutta (2015) and Kalyani University (2017). Like his predecessor Rabindranath Tagore, Joy Goswami is a living testimony of self-nurtured growth without punctilious education.

Introvert by nature, Joy Goswami began writing poetry at a very early age, though, he wasn't confident of his style. Gradually his poetries found their way to the pages of various little magazines, culminating eventually onto the poetry page of 'Desh' (Nation) magazine, the epitome of literature in West Bengal. In 1977, at the age of 23, Joy Goswami published his first collection of poetries, 'Christmas O Sheeter Sonetguchchho' (Sonnets of Christmas and Winter). This book brought him critical acclaim and he never had to doubt his creativity ever again. Perhaps poetry lovers were eagerly waiting for a new style of poetry and as soon as they were served with Joy Goswami's poetries, Joy became an instant celebrity.

Through his sensuousness and acutely scrutinized word application, Joy Goswami innovated a different intricacy of poetry for the Bengali poetry readers. He is a wizard of using juxtaposed imageries. Whether a poetry of love or a poetry against the ruling class, his writings are equally fierce in both. The flavor, the taste, the purport, the charm, the wit and the ultimate pleasure of reading a poetry are exuded in Joy Goswami's penmanship till its last word. Undoubtedly, he remains unparalleled. In fact a first reading of Joy Goswami's poetry glues a reader to his poetry, but to savor its inherent realm, a second or third reading becomes desirable.

This is evident in his novels as well. Joy Goswami's novels and stories become no less of a verse in their prose form. Besides Jibanananda Dash and Kamalkumar Majumdar, no other novelist so far has structured a story with such poetic aroma. Joy Goswami reflects a sense of self-discipline through the leanness in his creations where he doesn't waste even one extra word, culminating into a creation where each word is deeply penetrative. His essays are 'elaborate to the point' where every word takes the readers into the deepest layers of its essence.

Following his rise to glory as one of the most read poets, Joy Goswami worked as the editor of prestigious 'Desh' magazine for some time. Later he joined 'Songbaad Pratidin' (News Daily). Currently he is the chair of the state government run 'Nazrulteertho' (named after Kazi Nazrul Islam. Teertha means a place for pilgrimage).

In his poetry 'Why I am Rayless or Keno Aami Andhokaar", the poet eloquently shares his complex thoughts surrounding a couple's relationship. The contrast and dysfunctionality of human connection are reflected in this poetry. Yet an eternal optimism prevails through agony, confusion and disenchantment.

Joy Goswami has received numerous awards and recognitions including Ananda Puraskar (Ananda Award) twice (1990 and 1998), and Saahitya Academy Award (Academy of Literature) in 2000. In 2012, he was conferred with Banga-Bhusan title by the government of West Bengal.

Two of his writings, 'Jaaraa Bristitey Bhijechhilo' (Ones who Soaked in the Rain) and 'Saajhbaatir Roopkathaaraa' (Fairy-Tales of Saajhbaati) (Saajhbaati is a female name where saajh means evening and baati means a lamp) have been adopted into feature length films. Joy Goswami himself appeared as a poet in a movie titled, 'Sob Choritro Kaalponik' (All Characters are Fictitious) directed by famous film director Rituparno Ghosh.

Joy Goswami is married to his wife Kaberi Goswami since 1994.